Humanizing Institutions for the Aged

Humanizing Institutions for the Aged

Lee H. Bowker
The University of
Wisconsin—Milwaukee

LexingtonBooks
D.C. Heath and Company
Lexington, Massachusetts
Toronto

*In memory of Millard Price Thomas and
Freddie Alice Thomas,
who inspired this project, and much else.*

Library of Congress Cataloging in Publication Data

Bowker, Lee Harrington.
  Humanizing institutions for the aged.

  Includes index.
  1. Old age homes—United States. 2. Aged—Institutional care—United
States. I. Title.
HV1461.B68   362.6'1'0973   81–47977
ISBN 0–669–05209–4   AACR2

Published simultaneously in Canada

Printed in the United States of America

International Standard Book Number: 0–669–05209–4

Library of Congress Catalog Card Number: 81–47977

Contents

List of Figures
and Tables

Preface

I first became interested in institutions for the aged when visiting my wife's grandparents, Millard and Freddie Thomas, in their retirement apartment. They lived in an opulent facility that required new residents to buy their apartments (with ownership remaining in the name of the corporation) at exceedingly high prices, plus make sizable monthly payments for maid service, food service, and institutional upkeep. The institution was highly permeable yet guarded around the clock to keep the residents secure from unwanted intruders. It included its own medical unit but did not attempt to provide a full range of skilled-care nursing-home services in-house. The dining room, on a large lake and with an unobstructed view of the mountains, was fully staffed with waiters and waitresses and served high-quality food. A model facility in every way, this geriatric institution was nevertheless viewed by many of its residents in the same way that prisoners view maximum-security correctional institutions. Amazingly, I heard some of the same phrases used by elderly professionals and their survivors to describe the food, the administration, and other elements in this elegant facility that I had become acquainted with while directing the Social Therapy Program (a rehabilitation program for violence-prone drug abusers) at the Washington State Penitentiary.

How could this be? My sociological training provided me with an answer worth testing. Both facilities, no matter how different, were total institutions and, as such, were dominated by the effects of institutional totality as described by Erving Goffman in his book, *Asylums.* Although differences between the institutions and their resident populations had some impact on institutional life, many facets of institutional totalism overcame these differences.

The study reported in this book began as a comparison between prisons and geriatric institutions, changed into a comparison among geriatric institutions (at which point it was funded by the NRTA-AARP Andrus Foundation), and then metamorphosed into an investigation of humanization strategies in institutions for the aged. This book contains the remnants of these earlier project orientations and does not come to focus squarely on the investigation of humanization strategies until chapter 5. My interests in the field of gerontology are continuing to become more focused, with my current work revolving around the development of the humanization audit that is outlined in chapter 6.

This project could not have been completed without the marvelous efforts put forth by project staff members. Joan Dinan did the first draft of the bibliography and the direct observations in the geriatric facilities, as well as making many other contributions to the reports produced by the project. Dorothy Brostowicz was the project secretary, MaryAnn Riggs produced this book and other lengthy project manuscripts on the word-processing system, and Robin Hauser typed the bibliography. The administrators, staff, and residents of the four Milwaukee-area geriatric institutions bent over backward to welcome us into their homes and workplaces. At no time did they obstruct our observations in any way. The staff of the NRTA-AARP Andrus Foundation, which generously funded the project, was most supportive of the project's goals and showed admirable flexibility in its willingness to permit me to change certain details of the grant proposal after it was funded so that it would have a more-positive focus. As always, I must apologize to my wife, Dee, and children, Jessica and Wendy, for the weekends, afternoons, and evenings of family time that were lost to this project.

1

The Current State of Knowledge on Humanization and Dehumanization in Institutions for the Aged

Exact statistics on the use of residential institutions for the aged in the United States are not available. However, a recent California study found that 39 percent of a probability sample of the aged stayed in a convalescent hospital or nursing home at least once before their deaths. Slightly more than one in every seven individuals spent at least six months in an institution during the last years of life (Vicente, Wiley, and Carrington 1979). Assuming that these figures are fair approximations for the whole of U.S. society, we can see that the quality of life in nursing homes and similar residential institutions for the aged is a problem of major significance.

Until the mid–1970s, little attention had been given to topics such as the social organization of institutions for the aged; factors associated with variations in the residents' quality of life, morbidity, mortality, and mental functioning; and humanizing influences in these institutions. Considering the current rise in the number of people over 65 years of age, and the parallel increase in the national population of nursing-home residents, it is essential that a major research effort be carried out in the 1980s to further our understanding of these and related topics.

The nursing-home industry is already overregulated. Wisconsin nursing homes are subject to more than 1,500 state and federal regulations (Gustafson et al. 1980), of which 40 percent are duplicative (Wisconsin State Department of Health and Social Services 1977). Despite this governmental involvement in the operation of nursing homes, comparatively little effort has been expended to assure staff attention to the fully human needs of the residents in these institutions. Furthermore, little effort has been made to make government nursing-home-inspection reports available to consumers (Butler 1974). Government regulations too often follow the lead of medical-model opinion leaders such as the Joint Commission on Accreditation of Hospitals, whose *Accreditation Manual for Long Term Care Facilities* (1979) devotes approximately 90 percent of its standards to medical-model variables, with only a few pages reserved for patient/resident activities (four standards), patient/resident rights and responsibilities (four standards), and

1

spiritual services (one standard). The social-services standards show little awareness that they refer to living human beings rather than to objects.

Although government regulations often have had an antihumanization effect, they have been rather successful in promoting the medical needs of the residents. What then develops in institutions for the aged is best understood in terms of Maslow's (1968) need hierarchy. When basic physical needs are met, attention becomes focused on higher-level system needs—those associated with the concept of humanization. Nursing-home residents are capable of having peak experiences and reaching the highest level of self-actualization despite their physical infirmities.

The overall problem examined in this study is that institutions for the elderly are not as fully humanized as they might be given the resources at hand, and as they ought to be, given the constitutional standards and moral precepts of U.S. society. This point has been eloquently made in dozens of publications by social scientists (such as Stannard 1973), government bodies (U.S. Senate 1975), health-care administrators (Vladeck 1980), and writers of popular exposés (Garvin and Burger 1968).

When these authors cry out that life in nursing homes is dehumanizing, what precisely do they mean? Dictionary definitions of humanization avoid the issue by merely saying that it is the process of making something more humane or endowing it with human characteristics, and few scholarly definitions are any better. An outstanding exception to this generalization is Howard's (1975) conceptual view of humanization and dehumanization in health care. His definitions are so eloquent, and his arguments so persuasive, that we adopted his conception of humanization as a starting point for our investigation.

Howard (1975) proposes eight necessary and sufficient conditions for humanized health care. Three of these conditions are ideological in nature, three are structural, and the remaining two are affective. Increasing values on these eight dimensions increases the humanization of nursing-home residents, and decreasing values on these dimensions decreases their humanization. *Dehumanization* is simply a summary term for net decreases in the values of the humanization dimensions. Howard's eight dimensions are as follows:

1. *Inherent worth.* Human beings are objects of value, to themselves if not to others. . . . If persons are forced to prove their worth, . . . the burden of proof is dehumanizing.

2. *Irreplaceability.* We are unique and irreplaceable. When people are stereotyped and treated in terms of commonalities rather than differences, dehumanization can logically follow.

3. *Holistic selves.* At any given moment the sum total of a person's experience influences that person's feelings, attitudes, and actions. . . .

The patient's whole may be so fragmented that his or her problems become exclusive concerns of multiple practitioners who do not even communicate with one another.

4. *Freedom of action.* Humanized relationships are predicated on freedom of choice. Where the interaction is forced on participants or one or the other is bound against his will, the experience cannot be humanizing.

5. *Status equality.* Humanized relations involve equals on some level. If either sees his or her total self as superior or inferior to the other, the interaction cannot be fully humanizing.

6. *Shared decision making and responsibility.* [This concept] reflects the emerging ideology that all patients, regardless of education, have a right and perhaps a duty to participate as much as possible in decisions about their care.

7. *Empathy.* Humans have the ability to sympathize and identify with others. The more they compare themselves to others, the more easily they put themselves in others' shoes. . . . If practitioners contain their sympathy and avoid seeing the world from the vantage point of their patients, they cannot as readily understand the needs of those patients and appropriately respond to them as unique human beings.

8. *Positive affects.* Human beings are reservoirs and conveyors of emotion. Person-to-person interactions are most likely to involve emotional commitments because reciprocity and empathy can occur. [pp. 73–84]

Three Seminal Works on Institutions for the Aged as Total Institutions

The theoretical roots of the study of homes for the aged as total institutions can be found in Goffman's essay "On the Characteristics of Total Institutions" in his book, *Asylums* (1961), and Henry's study of three institutions for the aged in his volume, *Culture against Man* (1963). According to Goffman, total institutions are social organizations in which all elements of human life occur in the same place and under the same authority. An individual in a total institution does everything with a group of other institutional residents, all of whom are doing the same thing at the same time under a tight schedule imposed by some higher authority. All activities are rationally organized in the service of the institution's goals rather than the goals or needs of the residents. Among the valuable concepts developed by Goffman are disculturation, mortifications, "looping," the privilege system, inmate adaptations, the "sad tale," and the cycle of staff-resident contact and withdrawal. Two of the crucial mortifications suffered by residents in total institutions are the circulation of embarrassing facts about themselves by staff members, who may bring them up at any time, and the contamination of the self by undesirable material items and social relations. Looping occurs when a resident's defensive reaction to a mortification becomes an excuse for additional mortifications. In sad tales, residents make up stories to explain that their presence in the total institution is an accident, and does not reflect negatively on them.

In total institutions, residents are induced through a complex organization of privileges and punishments to conform to the house rules, the institutional regulations. They react to these pressures of institutional life in four ways: (1) withdrawal from the situation, (2) adoption of an intransigent line, (3) colonization, and (4) conversion to the staff's world view. Staff-client relations in total institutions tend toward the caste model of social stratification, which implies considerable social distance between the two groups as well as reciprocal negative stereotypes.

Goffman admits that total institutions differ and suggests three dimensions that are crucial in the degree of the totality of institutional life. These dimensions are extent of role differentiation, mode of recruitment, and permeability. Role differentiation refers to division of the residents into differing but interlocking social roles. Mode of recruitment varies among residents, some of whom freely enter homes for the aged, while others are forced by social, economic, and medical circumstances into entering these institutions. Permeability refers to the degree of contact between the institutionalized aged and members of the larger community.

Goffman's view of total institutions is extremely negative. His comments make clear that he judges the negative effects of living in total institutions to be so great that they overwhelm other aspects of institutional life. The general implication of his work is that many of these negative effects are due to structural properties that are common to all total institutions rather than to the actions of individual administrators.

Jules Henry (1963) discusses what he terms *human obsolescence* at three institutions for the aged: a municipal sanitarium and two private, profit-making institutions. One of the private nursing homes was comfortable and humane, the other was utterly inhuman, and the municipal sanitarium was in between. Henry describes the situation of the elderly at the municipal sanitarium as follows:

So they feel they're not human, and from this comes anguish that expresses itself in clinging. But silence is not the only form of dehumanizing communication to which these people are exposed. Empty walls, rows of beds close together, the dreariness of their fellow inmates, the bed pans, the odors, the routinization, all tell them they have become junk. Capping it all is the hostility of the patients to one another and the arbitrary movement from place to place like empty boxes in a storeroom. At the end is a degraded death. [p. 405]

Rosemont, the poorly funded private institution, reduced the elderly to the level of child-animals and kept them near to starvation in order to cut costs. Henry finds that:

> The transformations are possible in Rosemont only because of the acquiescence of the inmates; and this is obtained not only because the inmates are old and powerless, having been abandoned by their relatives and a miserly government but because, with one or two exceptions, they recognize that being obsolete they have no rights, because they understand that having nothing they are not going to get anything. [1963, p. 440]

The physical suffering found at Rosemont was not duplicated at the Tower nursing home, which served patients from the upper-middle class and above. This institution was clean, odorless, well organized, and well staffed. The physical needs of the residents at Tower were clearly met, with perhaps the only exception being that they were kept in bed for so many hours a day (for the convenience of staff members) that they became unnecessarily enfeebled over time. Despite this high level of physical care, life for the residents was less than ideal:

> The staff, though animated by *solicitude* and *kindliness* seems to maintain an attitude of *indulgent superiority* to the patients whom they consider *disoriented children,* in need of care, but whose confusion is to be brushed off, while their *bodily needs* are assiduously looked after. [Henry 1963, p. 474.]

The residents at Tower suffered a considerable amount of anxiety, punctuated by outbursts of petulance. They achieved no inner peace, and social life at the home was minimal. As a result, their social needs were so great that they reached out to the researcher in an attempt to continue human contact for as long as possible.

Henry's work suggests to us that although significant differences exist in the quality of physical care provided in diverse institutions for the elderly, other aspects of the old-age home as a total institution seem to be fairly uniform across institutional types. At the same time that Henry's eloquent descriptions depress us, they offer hope for, if culture triumphs over the needs of individuals even up to the point of death, then it can also be used to enrich the lives of the institutionalized aged.

Gubrium's study, *Living and Dying at Murray Manor* (1975), extends Henry's analysis, using a strictly phenomenological methodology that allowed him to record the activities, behavior, and opinions in the words of the clients and staff rather than in preformed categories and then to present them to the reader in an organized and intelligible fashion. Gubrium found that staff members used clientele lore and personal anecdotes to construct typifications of residents such as "perfectly confused persons" and "totally disoriented patients" (1975, p. 64). These typifications were then used to legitimize staff actions. Resident complaints, moreover, especially when they disrupted normal work routines, were often presented in such a way as to appear to stem from the personal problems of the residents themselves, rather than any inadequacies in staff performance. Gubrium notes, for example, that "a person who screams in rage at waiting for his food may be said to be *disoriented.* One who throws dishes or walks about in anger is *agitated* or *confused.*" (1975, p. 130).

The type of territoriality often evidenced by inmates of other total institutions existed among the elderly residents of Murray Manor. Gubrium states that even the officially public areas of Murray Manor were broken up into unofficial private places during certain times of the day. This territoriality was reinforced by patient cliques organized around alertness, length of time in the home, or perhaps common interests. Not only did these cliques guard their territory but also they served to confer status on member residents and demean nonclique members. Among these cliques, as well as among the resident population in general, food was a major topic of discussion. In fact, the residents' sarcastic tales about the awful food in the institution paralleled the staff's definitions of crazy resident behavior. The retelling of these food-related tales also served to reinforce the residents' sense of shared group identity by documenting the extent to which they shared a common world view.

Gubrium's methodology gently acquaints us with the nature of living in a total institution without either muckraking or using psychologistic scaling devices. More than any other publication on nursing homes, *Living and Dying at Murray Manor* helps us to understand that the environment of the institutionalized aged is largely a corollary of the structure and culture of these homes seen as total institutions.

Elaborations of Basic Insights

A number of other writers have conceptualized homes for the aged as total institutions. For example, Alders finds that homes for the aged bear "an uncomfortable resemblance to a camp for displaced persons" (1961, p. 946). The muckraking literature on homes for the aged gives us endless examples of the dehumanization and degradation that occur in these institutions. Unfortunately, authors such as Fontana (1978), Garvin and Burger (1968), Mendelson (1974), and Moss and Halamandaris (1977) tend to place the blame on individual administrators and staff members rather than to carry out a structural analysis of the effects of organizing the homes as total institutions.

There are numerous studies that can be adduced to show that the muck-rakers' simplistic analysis of individual culpability falls far short of a comprehensive explanation of the deficiencies of homes for the aged. As an example of this, Filer and O'Connell (1964) found that the behavioral performance of aged subjects was directly related to the degree of stimulation and presence of definite expectancies in the social environment. Melbin (1969) found that the presence of professional treatment personnel and clinical trainees who were receptive to the revelation of symptoms was associated with a high level of symptom-relevant behavior whose occurence was presumably reinforced by the reaction of the clinical staff members. Perhaps more important than institutional studies such as these is the behavioral comparison of a real and a mock nursing home by Wigdor, Nelson, and Hickerson (1977). Even a time period as short as forty-eight hours was sufficient to allow volunteer college students playing the roles of staff and residents to take on some of the characteristics known to be typical of these roles in total institutions. The pseudoresidents showed changes in submissiveness, withdrawal, introversion, complaining, and abusive language, while the pseudostaff members showed changes in the abuse of power, domination, and rigidity of rule enforcement. This study offers convincing evidence of the power of social roles as played in total institutions to quickly modify the behavior of participants in those institutions regardless of their personal characteristics.

Set against the studies that view homes for the aged as a class of total institutions are the studies that differentiate between institutions, such as those by Bennett (1963), Sherman (1972), and Coe (1965). Sherman compared six types of housing facilities for the aged; a retirement hotel, an urban high rise, a life-care home, and retirement villages at three different income levels. She found that the degree of satisfaction with retirement housing expressed by her subjects varied according to proximity, security, balance of independence and dependence, an optimum level of segregation by age, the degree of financial commitment required, psychological readiness to enter the facility, the provision of basic creature comforts, satisfaction with relatives and reference groups, and the degree of alienation or social integration experienced. Sherman did not pay much attention to the topic of total institutions, and many of the sites she included in her study really were not total institutions in any sense of the term. The primary value of her study for our purposes is in the information it gives us about what appear to be nondehumanizing ways of housing the relatively wealthy aged who are still physically and mentally able to live independently. In contrast, Coe and Bennett both direct their attentions specifically to the concept of total institutions. Coe tested the hypothesis that the degree of depersonalization in homes for the aged varies directly with the severity of the total characteristics of the institution. He compared a nursing home, a public institution, and a special unit in a large, private general hospital, finding that the clients evinced much "anxiety of the future, fear of and anger at unfulfilled kinship expectations, increasing dependence, and attempts to salvage some positive affect toward self" (1965, p. 241). In addition, they suffered from the phenomenon of group self-hatred, and all of these negative effects were more pronounced the more totalistic the institution.

Bennett (1963) analyzed the degree of totality of institutions for the aged into ten dimensions: duration of residence for which the institution was designed, orientation of activities, scheduling of activities, provisions made for dissemination of normative information, provisions for allocation of staff time for observations of behavior of inmates, type of sanction system, personal property, decision making about use of personal property, pattern of recruitment, and residential pattern. In a later research report, Bennett and Nahemow (1965) revealed that behavioral expectations were both minimal and vague in institutions high on the ten criteria of totality, clear but minimal in institutions low in totality, and considerably stronger in institutions of medium totality. The classification of institutions by level of care in a recent book by Manard, Woehle, and Heilman (1977) reminds us that the degree of institutional totality is not independent of the health-care needs of its residents. Those institutions serving people with higher levels of health-care needs are, on the average, considerably more totalistic than institutions serving clients with relatively low health-care needs. The ethnographies of a retirement hotel by Teski (1979) and a slum hotel for the elderly by Stephens (1976) show how the elderly poor who still have the power of ambulation maintain their freedom with great vigor. These individuals would clearly resist being relocated to a more-totalistic institution until forced to do so by physical infirmity. Another dimension that is potentially confounding with the degree of institutional totality is cost per resident per day, which presumably reflects the wealth and class backgrounds of the residents to some degree. Lawton tells us that the curse of poverty extends beyond the point of institutionalization, for "there are two radically different systems of care for the institutionalized older people—one for the poor and one for the relatively affluent" (1978, p. 113). Much has been written about the system of institutional care for the aged who are poor, but almost nothing is known about institutions for the wealthy aged. One of the few pieces on this subject in the literature is a chapter in Garvin and Burger's book, *Where They Go To Die: The Tragedy of America's Aged.* They describe cooperative housing for the aged in Montana, Oregon, Ohio, and San Diego in which entrance fees ranged as high as $37,000 in the mid-1960s. In their words, "contrasted with the abject misery and isolation of many oldsters in homes for aged, these affluent few present a picture of a social caste system on a grand scale" (1968, p. 145). As it happens, Garvin and Burger are so horrified at the affluence of these homes that they neglect to examine the possibility that totalistic-institutional characteristics exist in even these luxurious surroundings.

The Debate on the Effects of Institutionalization on the Aged

The scientific literature on geriatric institutions contains an extensive debate as to the effects of institutionalization. On the negative side, Vail (1966) goes so far as to support Barton's thesis that institutionalization produces a genuine neurosis that has the characteristics of loss of contact with the outside world; enforced idleness; bossiness of medical and nursing staff; loss of personal friends, possessions, and personal events; the use of drugs; a ward atmosphere; and loss of prospects outside the institution. Posner (1974) argues that privileges and rewards in homes for the aged are given out in inverse proportion to the degree of mental and physical competence displayed by the residents. Although outsiders tend to define admission to a home for the aged as evidence of incompetency, institutional staff at the geriatrics center studied by Posner defined the more-competent clients as unproblematic and largely left them alone when they were admitted. The best facilities and the greatest amount of attention from the staff members were given to those who were judged to be least competent. Therefore, the relatively healthy elderly are seen as being incompetent to live in the outside world but as being too competent to live in a home for the aged. It seems that they lose no matter where they are or what they do (Posner 1974).

Lieberman (1969) summarized the effects of institutionalization on the behavior of the aged, concluding that some of the negative effects associated with institutionalization are undoubtedly due to selection but that the evidence for selection is not strong enough to explain away all of the noxious effects associated with living in a total institution. Lieberman found that although some institutions were really better than others, many of the institutional characteristics that were instrumental in influencing the behavior of residents were shared by all institutions for the aged. He believes that "these common characteristics may be more salient in producing negative influences than those characteristics that differentiate one institution from another" (Lieberman 1969, p. 336). A study by Townsend (1962) shows that many of these negative institutional effects are as prevalent in England and Wales as they are in the United States. He found that the institutionalized aged were much more likely to report being often or sometimes lonely than similar surveys of the elderly living at home. Relatively few of them made friends with other residents in their institutions so they really did not balance the loss of many outside relationships with the creation of a new set of relationships that were home based. There was much reserve, suspicion, and even hostility between the institutional residents, and there were very few cases of close associations between residents and staff members. Other problems discussed by Townsend include the loss of privacy and identity and the collapse of powers of self-determination.

Suggestions for Improvements in the Quality of Life of Nursing-Home Residents

The literature on institutions for the aged also includes a number of suggestions for alleviating some of the negative effects of institutionalization. For example, Brickel discusses the use of cat mascots with a hospital-based geriatrics population. He found that the "mascots were effective in increasing patient responsiveness, giving patients a pleasurable experience, enhancing the treatment milieu, and helping keep patients in touch with reality" (1979, p. 372).

If relationships with cats are so therapeutically useful in homes for the aged what could be done if we fostered relationships with other human beings? Euster (1971) recommends that loneliness, friendlessness, and anxiety be combated by forming orientation groups for residents newly admitted to an institution, followed by living-and-learning groups that continue throughout the institutional stay of the individual. Since Smith and Bengtson found that family relationships were strengthened rather than weakened by institutionalization, they logically concluded that "the focus of the institution can become *service to families, not to isolated individuals*" (1979, p. 446). In fact, McMeekin (1977) advocates family involvement through every step of the nursing-home experience. Families, she feels, should participate in the decision-making process involving nursing-home selection and placement, the resident's transition and adjustment to the home, and the entire scope of activities in the home. Romney (1962) also perceives some type of family involvement as essential to the well-being of the nursing-home resident and recommends that nursing homes actively work to maintain positive family relationships, repair deteriorating ones, and substitute staff or volunteer relationships when family relationships are nonexistent. Holzman and Sabel (1968) indicate that programs to foster close ties between staff and residents can result not only in improved resident morale but also in improved staff morale.

Perhaps the best method of fostering interpersonal interaction in total institutions is to provide a wide variety of activities for the residents and then to encourage them to participate in these activities. Kahana (1973) points out that this implies allowing residents to participate in activities that may involve some degree of risk rather than continually sheltering them as much as possible. Permitting some interpersonal conflict between residents, rather than acting to suppress every sign of disagreement, may also be necessary as conflict can be the first step in the formation of primary groups that can be very supportive to residents (Jones 1972).

Routh (1968) presents one of the few systematic treatments of activity programs for nursing-home residents that exists in the literature. His categorization of these activities includes informational lectures, quiet table games, arts, crafts and hobbies, social events, musical events, performing groups from outside the nursing home, classes, and outdoor activities. Manard, Woehle, and Heilman (1977) argue, however, that the kinds of activities made available to elderly institutional residents are not equally attractive to all. Activities are usually more consistent with the past experiences of middle-class residents than residents from blue-collar and unskilled manual jobs, and they are also more consistent with the previous activities of women than men. Therefore, the acceptability of these activities to institutional residents and the correlation between activity provision and resident satisfaction is likely to vary according to the sex and class composition of the resident population in any given institution.

Some types of program opportunities seem particularly valuable in improving the quality of life for the elderly in nursing homes. For example, providing residents with opportunities for choice and responsibility seems to have many beneficial results. Langer and Rodin (1976) describe an experiment in which members of an experimental group of nursing-home residents were encouraged to make decisions for themselves, were provided with decision-making opportunities, and were given responsibility for the care of something besides themselves. Compared to a control group, these residents showed an increase in mental alertness and more active participation in nursing-home life. McClannahan and Risley (1973) propose, on the basis of their research, that providing a shopping activity within the nursing home is a fruitful way of promoting choice and decision making. Milieu therapy described by Gottesman (1973), Brink (1980), and others also attempts to foster decision making and creative problem solving among the elderly through environmental manipulation and the alteration of the institutional context. Milieu therapy involves changing attitudes of staff, families, and residents so that the latter no longer view themselves as dependent patients but rather as responsible persons who can do things for themselves and others.

Kalson (1976) sees service to others as a way of counteracting the loss of self-esteem that can occur in institutionalized elderly as a result of the loss of meaningful social roles. He describes an experiment in which elderly residents engaged in a program of social interaction with mentally retarded adults. He notes that the elderly participants improved in morale and in their patterns of social interaction.

The physical design of the institution can also provide residents with more control over their own lives. Koncelik (1976) shows how design features of both public and private areas can either foster resident control and sociability or inhibit both.

Institutionalization, insofar as it fosters loss of control over the social and environmental world, produces a discrepancy for the elderly individual between the worlds of past and present. Hence, new coping mechanisms are required (Adams 1979). Reminiscence and life-review therapy have been proposed as effective ways for the elderly to come to terms with unresolved past conflicts and encroaching dissolution and death. Lewis and Butler (1974) indicate that life-review therapy can take many forms—for example, a written or taped autobiography, pilgrimages, reunions, studies in gene-alogy, scrapbooks, photograph albums, and written summations of the individual's life's work. Others have suggested poetry reading and writing (Kelen 1980) and music (Phillips 1980) as fruitful ways of encouraging healthy reminiscing.

Depression, a common problem in the elderly because of the many losses associated with aging, seems to be exacerbated by institutionalization (Green 1979). Active intervention in the form of counseling and group ther-apy appears to ameliorate this depression and to have the added benefit of forestalling staff depression. The availability of counseling takes on an added importance for the elderly because so many in nursing homes are approaching death (Kastenbaum and Candy 1973) and need help in working through grief.

In contrast to these negative views of institutionalization, a number of scientists have offered evidence that either institutionalization is not as negative an experience as it appears at first or the negative effects observed are due more to dislocations upon entrance into an institution than to the totalistic characteristics of the institution. Lieberman (1969) offers the opin-ion that there appear to be more negative effects associated with entrance into institutions than with long-term institutional residence. In an earlier publication, Lieberman and Lakin (1963) described the trauma of insti-tutional entrance and found that women experienced this as primarily a rejection by their children and an implied rejection by society, while men experienced a greater feeling of discontinuity and interpreted institutional entrance in terms of a loss of past potency. In related studies, Anderson (1965) concluded that the negative effects of institutionalization could be mitigated by a continued high level of social interaction among residents and between residents and significant others outside of the institution; Ben-nett and Nahemow (1965) discovered that successful socialization within the institution was related to the degree of isolation experienced by the residents before institutional entry; and Dick and Friedsam (1964) found that resi-dents whose last living arrangement was with an intimate family member were much less likely to be satisfied with life in an institution than those residents who were previously socially isolated.

Two recent studies constitute additional serious attacks on the concept of institutionalization as a necessarily negative experience for the aged. Zemore and Eames (1979), for example, compared the residents of homes for the aged with a control group of those currently on institutional waiting lists, finding that no significant difference existed in the symptoms of depression between these two groups. Both of these groups reported more physical symptoms of depression than a control group of young adults, but there were no differences between the age groups in the cognitive or affective symptoms of depression. These results seriously bring into question the idea that the totalistic character of institutions for the elderly fosters depression. Perhaps one reason why the institutionalized elderly were not found to be more depressed than the noninstitutionalized elderly was that only those who had been in homes for more than a year were included in the institionalized sample, thus ruling out any possibility of transition effects.

Approaching the question of the negativity of institutional effects from a different direction, Smith and Bengtson (1979) found that the institutionalized elderly were not abandoned and isolated from their families. They found negative changes in social relationships with other family members to have occurred in only about 10 percent of the families studied. More-common patterns were renewed and strengthened closeness or a continuation of family closeness. Why would the family members become closer after one of them became institutionalized? The most commonly cited reason was the decrease in preadmission strains suffered by the family because of the needs of the elderly person. Other factors mentioned included improvements in the health of the institutionalized person due to superior health care, being able to enjoy time spent with the resident instead of always devoting all energies to the physical task of personal maintenance, and improved dispositions of the elderly that were associated with their forming new friendships within the institutions.

Three recent developments in the worlds of practice and scholarship have important implications for meeting the human needs of nursing-home residents. The first of these is the sheltered-care-environment scale (SCES) that has been developed by Moos and his associates (1979) at Stanford University. Based on his earlier work in other institutional settings, the SCES allows us to measure the social climate of institutions for the aged. The SCES contains seven subscales organized into three groups. Cohesion and conflict are relationship dimensions; independence and self-exploration are personal-growth dimensions; and organization, resident influence, and physical comfort are dimensions of system maintenance and change. Five of these dimensions deal directly with humanization, and the other two are related to the subject. In giving us a ready-to-use scale, Moos and his co-workers have made it possible for every nursing-home administrator to gauge the level of some of the most important humanization-related variables in their own institutions without requiring either extensive specialized training or the hiring of outside consultants.

The second recent development in the humanization of institutions for the aged is the Gustafson et al. (1980) work on measuring the quality of care in a sample of Wisconsin nursing homes. This study has resulted in a facility-screening model that is much simpler and easier to administer than the complex of state and federal regulations that are currently used to certify nursing homes in Wisconsin. This facility-screening model contains eleven major criteria, which are broken down into numerous components that are used in evaluating institutions: philosophy, management, care management, resident-staff relationship, residents' condition, activities, safety of facility, staff, community ties, resident population, and professional ties. Fifty-six percent of the components of these dimensions appear to have humanization content in areas such as "residents' strength and abilities (fostered versus ignored)," "communication between residents (interaction fostered by activities versus inhibited)," and "importance of community (encouragement of community involvement in home versus not encouraging it)" (Gustafson et al. 1980, p. 340).

The final development in the humanization of institutions for the aged is Nicholson's (1979) personalized-care model (PCM). She and her colleagues found that the institutional culture was destructive to nursing-home residents at the biophysical and psychocultural levels because of its reliance upon the medical model. The encouragement of dependence on staff members and deculturation (or role diminishment) were catalysts in the deterioration process. Services were delivered to the residents as a class rather than as unique persons, and treatment plans were not written from the perspective of the resident as a whole person.

As an alternative to this unsatisfactory state of affairs, the PCM focuses staff attention on the person rather than the task. It sensitizes staff members to the role transitions that nursing-home residents undergo, and it gives their human needs as much emphasis as their biological-system needs. Among the changes necessary to implement the PCM are holistic, multidisciplinary training for staff members; training that builds in implementation techniques and strategies; and a number of changes in the system of the institution. The required systemic changes include: (1) stabilization of staff to unit, patient, and shift; (2) having a primary helper designated for each resident; (3) using aides rather than nurses as primary helpers; (4) replacing resident-staff-dependency relationships with helping relationships; (5) integrating therapeutic activities into the daily life of the unit, ward, or family group; (6) expanding the social networks of the residents by creating interest groups facilitated by the primary helpers; and (7) involving the entire staff in implementing treatment plans.

References

Adams, Eleanor B. *Reminiscence and Life Review in the Aged: A Guide for the Elderly, Their Families, Friends, and Service Providers.* Denton: Center for Studies in Aging, North Texas State University, 1979.

Alders, William. "The Idea of a Home for the Aged: A Re-Appraisal." *Journal of the American Geriatrics Society* 9 (1961):943–946.

Anderson, Nancy N. "Institutionalization, Interaction, and Self-Conception in Aging." In *Older People and Their Social World,* edited by Arnold M. Rose and Warren A. Peterson, pp. 245–257. Philadelphia: F.A. Davis, 1965.

Bennett, Ruth. "The Meaning of Institutional Life." *Gerontologist* 3 (1963):117–125.

Bennett, Ruth, and Nahemow, Lucille. "The Relations between Social Isolation, Socialization and Adjustment in Residents of a Home for the Aging." In *Mental Impairment in the Aging,* edited by M.P.Lawton, pp. 88–105. Philadelphia: Maurice Jacobs, 1965.

Berdes, Ceilia. *Social Services for the Aged Dying and Bereaved in International Perspective.* Washington, D.C.: International Federation on Aging, 1978.

Brickel, Clark M. "The Therapeutic Roles of Cat Mascots with a Hospital-Based Geriatric Population: A Staff Survey." *Gerontologist* 19 (1979):368–372.

Brink, T.L. "Milieu Therapy for the Institutionalized Aged: Psychotherapeutic and Economic Perspectives." *Long-Term Care and Health Services Administration Quarterly* 4 (1980):125–131.

Butler, Robert N. "The Nursing Home Cover-Up: Regulation Gaps and Other Dirty Tricks Played on Old People." *International Journal of Aging and Human Development* 5 (1974):295–297.

Coe, Rodney M. "Self-Conception and Institutionalization." In *Older People and Their Social World,* edited by Arnold M. Rose and Warren A. Peterson, pp. 225–243. Philadelphia: F.A. Davis, 1965.

Dick, Harry R., and Friedsam, Hiram J. "Adjustments of Residents of Two Homes for the Aged." *Social Problems* 11 (1964):282–290.

Euster, Gerald L. "A System of Groups in Institutions for the Aged." *Social Casework* 52 (1971):523–529.

Filer, Richard N., and O'Connell, Desmond D. "Motivation of Aging Persons." *Journal of Gerontology* 19 (1964):15–22.

Fontana, Andrea. "Ripping Off the Elderly: Inside the Nursing Home." In *Crime at the Top: Deviance in Business and the Professions,* edited by John Johnson and Jack Douglas, pp. 125–132. Philadelphia: Lippincott, 1978.

Garvin, Richard M., and Burger, Robert E. *Where They Go to Die: The Tragedy of America's Aged.* New York: Delacorte Press, 1968.

Goffman, Erving. *Asylums.* Garden City, N.Y.: Doubleday, 1961.

Gottesman, Leonard E. "Milieu Treatment of the Aged in Institutions." *Gerontologist* 13 (1973):23–26.

Green, Zoe E. *Depression in the Long-Term Care Facility.* Denton: Center for Studies in Aging, North Texas State University, 1979.

Gubrium, Jaber F. *Living and Dying at Murray Manor.* New York: St. Martin's Press, 1975.

Gustafson, David H.; Fiss, Charles J., Jr.; Fryback, Judy G.; Smelser, Peggy; and Hiles, Mary E. "Measuring the Quality of Care in Nursing Homes: A Pilot Study in Wisconsin." *Public Health Reports* 95 (1980):336–343.

Henry, Jules. *Culture against Man.* New York: Random House, 1963.

Holzman, Seymour, and Sabel, E.N. "Improving the Morale of the Patients and the Staff in a Geriatric Institution by a Supervised Visiting Program." *Gerontologist* 8 (1968):29–33.

Howard, J. "Humanization and Dehumanization of Health Care." In *Humanizing Health Care,* edited by J. Howard and A. Strauss. New York: Wiley, 1975, pp. 57–107.

Joint Commission on Accreditation of Hospitals. *Accreditation Manual for Long Term Care Facilities.* Chicago, Ill., 1979.

Jones, Dean C. "Social Isolation, Interaction, and Conflict in Two Nursing Homes." *Gerontologist* 12 (1972):230–234.

Kahara, E. "The Humane Treatment of Old People in Institutions." *Gerontologist* 13 (1973):282–289.

Kalson, Leon. "M*A*S*H, A Program of Social Interaction between Institutionalized Aged and Adult Mentally Retarded Persons." *Gerontologist* 16 (1976):340–348.

Kastenbaum, Robert, and Candy, Sandra E. "The 4% Fallacy: A Methodological and Empirical Critique of Extended Care Facility Population Statistics." *International Journal of Aging and Human Development* 4 (1973):15–21.

Kelen, Joyce G. "The Effects of Poetry on Elderly Nursing Home Residents." Ph.D. dissertation, University of Utah, 1980.

Koncelik, Joseph A. *Designing the Open Nursing Home.* Stroudsburg. Pa.: Dowden, Hutchinson and Ross, 1976.

Langer, Ellen J., and Rodin, Judith. "The Effects of Choice and Enhanced Personal Responsibility for the Aged: A Field Experiment in an Institutional Setting." *Journal of Personality and Social Psychology* 34 (1976):191–198.

Lawton, M.P. "Institutions and Alternatives for Older People." *Health and Social Work* 3 (1978):108–134.

Lewis, Myrna I., and Butler, Robert N. "Life-Review Therapy: Putting Memories to Work in Individual and Group Psychotherapy." *Geriatrics* 29 (1974):165–173.

Lieberman, Morton A. "Institutionalization of the Aging: Effects on Behavior." *Journal of Gerontology* 24 (1969):330–340.

Lieberman, Morton A., and Lakin, Martin. "On Becoming an Institutionalized Aged Person." In *Processes of Aging: Social and Physiological Perspectives,* vol. 1, edited by Richard H. Williams; C. Tibbits; and W. Donahue, pp. 475–503. New York: Atherton Press, 1963.

Manard, Barbara B.; Woehle, Ralph E.; and Heilman, James M. *Better Homes for the Old.* Lexington, Mass.: D.C. Heath, 1977.

Maslow, Abraham H. *Toward a Psychology of Being.* Princeton, N.J.: Van Nostrand Rinehold, 1968.

McClannahan, Lynn E., and Risley, Todd R. "A Store for Nursing Home Residents." *Nursing Homes* 22 (June 1973):10, 11, 29.

McMeekin, Betty. *Family Involvement in the Nursing Home Experience.* Denton: Center for Studies in Aging, North Texas State University, 1977.

Melbin, Murray. "Behavior Rhythms in Mental Hospitals." *American Journal of Sociology* 74 (1969):650–665.

Mendelson, Mary A. *Tender Loving Greed.* New York: Alfred A. Knopf, 1974.

Moos, Rudolf H.; Gauvain, Mary; Lemke, Sonne; Max, Wendy; and Mehren, Barbara. "Assessing the Social Environment of Sheltered Care Settings." *Gerontologist* 19 (1979):74–82.

Moss, Frank E., and Halamandaris, Val J. *Too Old, Too Sick, Too Bad: Nursing Homes in America.* Germantown, Md.: Aspen Systems, 1977.

Nicholson, Clara H. "Personalized Care in the Nursing Home: Problems and Practice." Paper presented at the Annual Meeting of the Gerontological Society, 1979.

Phillips, John R. "Music in the Nursing of Elderly Persons in Nursing Homes." *Journal of Gerontological Nursing* 6 (1980):37–39.

Posner, Judith. "Notes on the Negative Implications of Being Competent in a Home for the Aged." *International Journal of Aging and Human Development* 5 (1974):357–364.

Romney, Leonard F. "Extension of Family Relationships into a Home for the Aged." *Social Work* 7 (1962):31–34.

Routh, Thomas A. *Nursing Homes: A Blessing or a Curse.* Springfield, Il.: Charles C Thomas, 1968.

Sherman, Susan R. "Satisfaction with Retirement Housing: Attitudes, Recommendations and Moves. *Aging and Human Development* 3 (1972):339–366.

Smith, Kristen F., and Bengtson, Vern L. "Positive Consequences of Institutionalization: Solidarity between Elderly Parents and Their Middle-Aged Children." *Gerontologist* 19 (1979):438–447.

Stannard, Charles I. "Old Folks and Dirty Work: The Social Conditions for Patient Abuse in a Nursing Home." *Social Problems* 20 (1973): 329–341.

Stephens, Joyce. *Loners, Losers and Lovers.* Seattle: University of Washington Press, 1976.

Teski, Marea. *Living Together: An Ethnography of a Retirement Hotel.* Washington, D.C.: University Press of America, 1979.

Townsend, Peter. *The Last Refuge: A Survey of Residential Institutions and Homes for the Aged in England and Wales.* London: Routledge & Kegan Paul, 1962.

U.S. Senate, Special Committee on Aging. *Nursing Home Care in the United States: Failure in Public Policy.* Washington, D.C.: Government Printing Office, 1975.

Vail, David J. *Dehumanization and the Institutional Career.* Springfield, Il.: Charles C Thomas, 1966.

Vicente, Leticia; Wiley, James A.; and Carrington, R.A. "The Risk of Institutionalization before Death." *Gerontologist* 19 (1979):361–367.

Vladeck, D.C. *Unloving Care: The Nursing Home Tragedy.* New York: Basic Books, 1980.

Wigdor, Reubin M.; Nelson, Jack; and Hickerson, Elzie. "The Behavioral Comparison of a Real vs. Mock Nursing Home." *Gerontologist* 17(5, Part 2) (1977):133.

Wisconsin. State Department of Health and Social Services. "Final Report: Monitoring the Quality of Nursing Home Care." Madison, 1977.

Zemore, Robert, and Eames, Nancy. "Psychic and Somatic Systems of Depression among Young Adults, Institutionalized Aging and Non-institutionalized Aging." *Journal of Gerontology* 34 (1979):716–722.

2 Methodology and Descriptions of the Institutions Studied

Methodology

Three-hundred hours of direct observations were carried out in each of four institutions for the aged located in Milwaukee County. Following the precepts of social phenomenology more than any other methodological corpus, our intent was to record the world of the institutions as seen from the viewpoints of the actors living and working within them—the residents, direct-service staff members, and administrators. Each institution granted us twenty-four hour access to all institutional areas and activities. Observations were carried out as naturally and unobtrusively as possible although no attempt was made to disguise the observer's purpose in being present in the institution. No notes were taken in the presence of the residents, but they were written up in secluded rooms provided by the institutions or shortly after leaving the research sites.

Our study utilized no data-collection instruments in the usual sense of the word. Participant observation was carried out by spending many painstaking hours on-site and carefully recording the behavior and environment observed there. It was not sufficient to record behavior abstractly for the meaning of behavior rather than behavior itself is crucial to understanding the degree of totalism in homes for the aged (or any other human behavior). The participant observer must talk with clients to ascertain how they interpret their environment and what they mean by what they say and do. Triangulation was consistently followed in our study as the views of various residents and staff members were solicited with respect to the same subjects, events, behaviors, and problems.

In the place of formal data-collection instruments, participant observation demands a high degree of observational organization in the field and very careful data analysis outside the field setting. Procedures used in the field included the following items derived from Bogdan and Taylor's (1975) methodological treatment of field-research procedures:

Looking for key words in each subject's remarks,

Concentrating on the first and last remarks in each conversation,

Leaving the setting when as much had been observed as could be remembered accurately,

Recording notes as soon after the observation session as possible,

Refraining from talking to anyone about observation sessions until the field notes had been recorded,

Picking up pieces of lost data after the initial recording session when appropriate.

As clients and staff members became more at home with the observer, they shed their official positions on nursing-home life and began to share their personal opinions and inner feelings. It was common for these opinions and feelings to be just the opposite of the official positions that had been taken in initial contacts with the observer. The researchers guaranteed complete anonymity to the institutions, staff members, and residents. While this was important to several of the administrators and professional staff members, other staff members quickly lost any concern with anonymity as they came to trust the observer. The residents were unconcerned about anonymity at any time during their contacts with the observer.

The four institutions were selected to fall from low to high on a continuum of organizational totality. In the original research design, sites were to be chosen so as to fill the cells of a two-by-two property space formed by the intersection of the dimensions of cost per resident per day (a rough index of the funding level of the institution and the socioeconomic status of the residents) and availability of activity programs fostering interpersonal action. It was assumed that institutions high on both dimensions would be low on institutional totality, that institutions low on both dimensions would be high on institutional totality, and that mixed cases would be intermediate between those two extremes on institutional totality. Unfortunately, it was found that, while considerable variation existed among institutions on the dimension of availability of activity programs fostering interpersonal interaction, little variation existed on cost per resident per day for comparable levels of services. This effect is largely produced by the low proportion of private-pay residents in Milwaukee-area nursing homes and the standard reimbursement rates that have been established by the state of Wisconsin. In order to obtain sizable differences on the variable of cost per resident per day, it was necessary to choose an institution offering a much lower level of services to the residents. This, of course, confounded service level and degree of resident infirmity with cost per resident per day, but it was still better than having all four institutions cluster together on the cost dimension.[1] The final sample therefore consisted of three nursing homes offering both skilled care and intermediate care to residents, plus a community-based residential facility that offered room and board plus a number of additional support services as needed. Table 2-1 summarizes the characteristics of these four institutions.

Table 2-1
Characteristics of the Institutions for the Aged Studied

Institution	Level of Programmed Social Interaction	Cost per Resident per Day
Hoover Home	Somewhat high	High ($59 private, $50 double for skilled care)
Truman Manor	Very low	Very low (no skilled care available, $10 private, $8 double for room and board)
Roosevelt Residence	Very high	Moderate ($50 private, $43 double for skilled care)
Eisenhower Care Center	Somewhat low	Moderate ($49 private, $47 double for skilled care)

The Institutions

To protect the identities of all the individuals and organizations participating in the study, we have given them pseudonyms. Any resemblance of these names to individuals or institutions in the Milwaukee area is purely coincidental.

Hoover Home

Hoover Home provides accommodations for approximately 250 residents, almost all of them in double rooms. Slightly more than 95 percent of the resident population is white, and approximately 67 percent are women. Almost all of the residents are on Medicaid. The institution makes available forty hours of occupational therapy per week, forty hours of physical therapy per week, and forty hours of remotivation therapy per week. These therapies are all provided by certified therapists. Although the institution does not employ a social worker with an MSW degree, four social workers with bachelor's degrees are on the staff. Chaplain services are provided on a volunteer basis by clergy and laypeople, usually biweekly.

All floors, drinking fountains, dining rooms, mirrors, light switches, and closets are wheelchair accessible. Residents are allowed to bring their own television sets, radios, bureaus, upholstered chairs, bedspreads, and wall decorations for use in their rooms. Special programs and activities provided in the institution include a bookmobile, arts and craft groups, shopping trips, cooking groups, discussion groups, organized games, picnics, sewing classes, movies, concerts, music therapy, reality-orientation groups, and a resident newspaper. A resident council is barely operational in the facility.

The institution houses residents on three floors; residents with the highest care needs are on the first floor, and those with the lowest level of care needs are on the third floor. A large lounge is used for religious activities as well as games and in-service training. Each of the three floors has three wings, with a large nursing station at the point of intersection of the wings, as well as a large resident lounge. Other resident lounges are also located on each floor, and some have television sets that are controlled from the nursing stations. The average level of physical infirmity among the residents is rather high, with more than two-thirds of the institutionalized population being in the skilled-care category. This high proportion of skilled-care residents prompts staff at Hoover Home to justify the hospitallike atmosphere of the institution.

Truman Manor

Truman Manor is not a nursing home. It is a community-based residential facility. As such, it is not the recipient of Medicaid funds. However, it is still largely government supported in that most of the residents pay their monthly charges with their social security checks. The population of Truman Manor fluctuated between 60 and 70 residents during the period of the study. Despite being located in an area of the city with a substantial minority population, only one of the residents was black and none was Hispanic. Approximately 60 percent of the residents were women. They occupied most of the first and all of the second floors of the building; the third floor was reserved for male residents.

In addition to the bedroom areas, the facility includes a dining room in the basement, three smoking and one non-smoking lounges, and various sparsely furnished activity rooms. A large yard with benches and trees is provided for comfortable outdoor recreation. Practically no institutional areas are easily accessible to residents in wheelchairs.

No therapy groups are provided by the very limited staff of the facility. Volunteers from the community and outreach workers provide a number of activities and services every week. The mobility of most of the residents allows them freely to come and go so that they are able to secure many services themselves in the external community.

Roosevelt Residence

This nursing home contains approximately 200 beds, almost all of them in double rooms. Two-thirds of the residents are women, and nearly all of them are white. Polish and German ethnic groups are heavily represented, and many residents come from a fairly small geographic area surrounding the institution. A good many of the residents enter the institution on a private-pay basis, which is in direct contrast to Hoover Home.

The institution provides fifty-six hours of occupational therapy per week, sixty-four hours of physical therapy per week, and sixteen hours of speech therapy per week, all of them by certified therapists. There are no social workers in a strict sense of the term. In their place are several social-service positions. Religious services are provided, on a consultation basis, four hours per week.

There is a resident council that is extremely active in the facility. Drinking fountains, dining rooms, and all floors, mirrors, light switches, and closets are wheelchair accessible. Residents are encouraged to bring their own wall decorations, bedspreads, upholstered chairs, bureaus, radios, and television sets for use in their rooms. Activities provided by the institution include monthly birthday parties and dinners, many celebrations on holidays, family breakfasts, community outings, a daily in-house radio station, a resident newspaper, movies, socials, and both indoor and outdoor sports activities. There are weekly religious services, and a chaplain serves as a consultant four hours a week.

The facility is built entirely on one floor, with two enclosed patios. There are also a number of lounges and activity rooms. The facility has been constructed to have ample space for visiting, and the rooms and hallways have been furnished so as to suggest a homelike atmosphere rather than an institutional atmosphere. The small store in the front lobby is completely staffed by residents.

Eisenhower Care Center

The Eisenhower Care Center is the only nonprofit facility studied. It houses just under 200 residents, more than half of them in double rooms and most of the remainder in triple rooms. Just over half of the resident population is female, which is a reflection of the fact that the institution was once limited to male residents, and it has not yet attained the high percentage of female residents that is usually found throughout the nursing-home industry. Irish and Polish residents are heavily represented in the institution, but there are no racial-minority residents at all.

Eisenhower Care Center provides thirty-two hours of occupational therapy per week, forty hours of physical therapy, eight hours of speech-therapy, and two hours of remotivation therapy, all by certified therapists. There is one social worker with a bachelor's degree but none with an MSW degree. Dining rooms, floors, and mirrors are wheelchair accessible, but drinking fountains, light switches, and closets are not. Residents are encouraged to bring their own radios and television sets, along with some pictures for the walls in their rooms. Other large personal items are forbidden. A resident council there is not very active in institutional affairs. Other activities and services provided by the institution include trips to concerts, museums, and shopping centers; luncheons; picnics; craft groups; and organized games.

The facility contains four floors and many long hallways. The residents live in the three upper floors, with the ground floor largely devoted to administrative offices. There is also a small annex that is not part of the facility proper. Residents living in the annex are essentially independent and become part of the nursing home home only when they join the institution for meals and to participate in selected social activities. Each floor has its own dining room, which is attractively decorated. Few activity rooms and other places are available for social activities as the institution was constructed before such concerns were considered to be important in architecture. In the absence of dayrooms, the nursing station, front lobby, and cafeteria (which is open to residents all day) assume great importance as centers for social interaction. The building is surrounded by spacious and beautiful grounds, but relatively few residents are able to make use of them because they have not been developed for wheelchair use.

In the next chapter, the physical descriptions of the institutions that have been presented here come to life as the roles played by the staff and residents are discussed. An identification of the major themes that are characteristic of life in Hoover Home, Truman Manor, Roosevelt Residence, and Eisenhower Care Center follows.

Note

1. Other variables also confound the meaning of cost per resident per day. For example, in proprietary nursing homes, the profit the corporation desires to make on the care of residents is affected by factors such as real-estate speculation and depreciation (Vladeck 1980; Shulman and Galanter 1976). The ratio of Title XIX to private-pay residents is also important as Title XIX allocates a certain amount of money for recreational activities, whereas the income generated by private-pay residents is not so allocated. Title XIX reimbursement rates, however, are insufficient to cover other resident costs. Hence, if a facility is compelled to fill beds with Title XIX residents, rather than suffer the income loss generated by empty beds, the rates paid by private-pay residents must escalate to make up the income deficiency (although this escalation is still lower than the rate rise that would occur if these beds were permitted to remain empty). Humanization is also affected if the Title XIX beds are filled with long-term psychiatric

and developmentally disabled residents as this can affect the whole thrust of the recreational programs.

References

Bogdan, Robert, and Taylor, Steven J. *Introduction to Qualitative Research Methods: A Phenomenological Approach to the Social Sciences.* New York: Wiley, 1975.

Shulman, David, and Galanter, Ruth, "Reorganizing the Nursing Home Industry: A Proposal." *Milbank Memorial Fund Quarterly/Health and Society* 54 (1976):129–143.

Vladeck, Bruce C. *Unloving Care: The Nursing Home Tragedy.* New York: Basic Books, 1980.

3 Residential Institutions for the Aged as Total Institutions

This chapter consists of three parts. The first section presents classifications of roles played by staff members and residents in the institutional environment. The second section outlines themes characteristic of the institutional environment as expressed by staff and residents, and the third section presents findings regarding the analogy between institutions for the aged and maximum-security prisons.

An Informal Typology of Roles

What follows is an informal typology of roles in that the types described are not mutually exclusive. This is true at both the level of the abstract, or ideal, representation of types and the real experience of the types as acted out and experienced in a specific institutional setting. These role types are behavioral, representational types, not classifications of individual actors seen holistically. For staff members, their official position within the organization is a crucial determinant of their behavior. For residents, there is no differentiation by position but instead by their reactions to institutionalization. The lack of mutual exclusivity among categories at the formal, logical level of analysis is further complicated by the way in which the types occur in the everyday life of geriatric institutions. At the empirical level of analysis, we see that some individuals hold more than one institutional position and therefore exhibit different types of behavior according to which position they are representing at a given point in time. Even more confusing, actors who play only a single, undifferentiated role in the life of the institution display elements of different behavioral types at different times, depending on the context of the social situation. For these reasons, it would be highly misleading to assume that behavior representative of a given type will consistently be displayed by individuals whose primary identification is with that particular type over an extended period of time and regardless of the characteristics of the immediate social environment.

Nurses

The most powerful social group in most institutions for the aged is the department of nursing. The nursing staff can be divided into top-level

27

supervisors led by the director of nursing, registered nurses (RNs), licensed practical nurses (LPNs), and nursing aides. The director of nursing and the top-level supervisors are best categorized together with other administrators; thus they are discussed later in this section. There are two basic types of RNs, both of which are well within the orbit of the medical model. Career geriatric nurses are RNs who developed a professional interest in geriatric nursing early in their careers and who are working in an institution for the aged as part of their unbroken line of career development. One young career geratric nurse describes her nursing interest in this way:

> I've always wanted to work with old people, ever since I was a little girl. After my first practice rotation, I knew geriatric nursing was for me. It's a real calling, and you have to be a different kind of nurse. There's such a variety of skills called for, and you have so much more responsibility—not so much kowtowing to doctors. Someday, geriatric nurses will be more respected![1]

The second type of RNs contains nurses who have retreated to geriatric institutions from positions in hospitals that they found to be too demanding or who resumed a nursing career after a long hiatus. They are more satisfied with working conditions in nursing homes because there is less pressure on them there than they experienced in hospitals. One nurse said

> I've been out of the field so long that I didn't want to try to catch up with all the new things hospital nurses are doing. Here, it's more like elderly pediatrics. It's more relaxed too, and I have a more-flexible schedule. With kids at home, that's important.

Unlike career geriatric nurses, these nurses perceive geriatric nursing as less demanding instead of more demanding than hospital work. They are less interested in geriatrics as a field than the career geriatric nurses, and some of them have less-positive attitudes toward work with geriatric residents than the career geriatric nurses.

LPNs differ from RNs in that the educational requirements are less stringent. Although this means that technical, professional competence may be lower in some areas, their competence in practical geriatrics may be greater than the competence of the RNs as the LPNs have more responsibility for most direct patient care than do the RNs. One type of LPN is the career geriatric LPN, who has the same characteristics as the career geriatric RN. The other two types of LPNs are college students and former nursing aides. College students may be with the facility for a relatively short period of time while they are completing their course work to become RNs, and they may or may not have occupational goals in the area of geriatrics. In any case, they are not highly institutionalized, and they live in the social world of the educational institution as well as the geriatric institution and their private lives.

It is not unusual for a nursing aide to complete the course work necessary to become an LPN over a period of years while working in a geriatric facility. Because they spend a number of years as nursing aides, these LPNs have a more-comprehensive view of the life of an institution for the aged than do those nurses who came to the institution as LPNs. One LPN asserted

> I used to be an aide. I know what really goes on here, despite what they say. I've got a lot of sympathy for the aides. If you're a good aide, you really work your tail off. You sure get to know the patients, too. Now if I want to know about a patient, I ask the aide.

Nursing Aides

Nursing aides can be classified in terms of their social background and their motivation for working. Many nursing aides work for money alone. Although salaries are low, they have few salable skills, and so they are forced to accept any work that they can find. Not surprisingly, the absentee and turnover rates are high among this group. Some are just filling in time until they can find or return to other employment. One young, black school dropout described her job in this manner:

> It's a job. As soon as the factory calls me back though I'm going. The money's better at the factory, and you don't have to work so hard. This is all right here, but I sure don't plan on spending the rest of my life cleaning up shit off of old people.

A second group of nursing aides, although in need of money just as much as the first group, is strongly motivated by humanistic values. In extreme cases, these nursing aides may even view their work in a geriatric institution as a calling. Most humanistically motivated nursing aides define their humanistic values in religious terms rather than in philosophical or social-welfare terms. These sentiments are more likely to be expressed in the nonprofit institutions sponsored by religious organizations than in state facilities or proprietary institutions. One older aide asserted

> I mean we're supposed to care about each other, aren't we? What's life all about if you don't serve others? I sure don't do this for money. You couldn't pay me enough to get me to do this work just for the money.

Since the nursing aides are usually paid close to the minimum wage, it is no surprise that many of them come from the lower reaches of the social order. Many of them are poor whites and minority-group members who have to fight hard to stay just above the poverty level. Some are the sole support of large families and work double shifts as often as possible or work part time in other nursing homes as regular staff or as pool help. Often they are tired and are irritable with their elderly charges, yet it is not unusual to hear some of the residents sympathize with the plight of these impoverished aides and excuse their irritability on the grounds that "they're so tired—they work so hard."

A very different group of nursing aides is composed of students who are working their way through college. The final group contains working-class housewives, some of whom have been unexpectedly displaced into the job market by the death of a spouse or divorce. A second subgroup of working-class housewives is in the job market temporarily rather than permanently, with the primary purpose of adding to the family income in order to cover the unusual expenses associated with their children's education or needs, a family illness, or a long-desired vacation. In response to being questioned about why she chose to work as a nursing aide, one exhousewife responded

> Braces—my son needed braces. My husband said that we either had to cut back or I had to go to work. This [facility] was right around the corner from where we live, so here I am. I had applied to work in the laundry, but they needed aides. I never dreamed that I'd be an aide. I had always thought that I wouldn't be able to stand it.

Table 3-1 displays the interaction between the social backgrounds of nursing aides and their motivation for working.

Nursing aides are not usually devoted to the medical model of service delivery. They may be dominated by it through the system of orders and

Table 3-1
Naturalistic Typology of Nursing Aides in Institutions for the Aged

Social Background	Motivation for Working	
	Money Alone	Humanistic Values and Money
Poor	NA_1	NA_2
College students	NA_3	NA_4
Working-class housewives, some displaced and some temporary	NA_5	NA_6

charts with which they are controlled by their supervisors in the nursing department, but this depends on the rigor with which these supervisors enforce their medical-model view of the operation of the institution. Also, the medical model may serve the practical interest of these aides in completing bed and body work. Since aides are most often judged by how quickly and efficiently they perform bed and body work, the accomplishment of this work becomes a major concern for them. The medical model may facilitate bed and body work as it tends to produce docility and compliance in the elderly, and docile and compliant people are far easier to care for than independent individuals who may challenge the authority of the aides and thus obstruct the bed and body work. Obviously those aides who combine a sense of humanistic values with the need for money in their motivation for working in geriatric institutions tend more toward the humanistic model of service delivery than the nursing aides who are working for money alone.

Figure 3-1 illustrates the point that nursing aides (as well as other staff groups in institutions for the aged) cannot all be arrayed on a continuum of interest ranging from high medical-model dominance to high humanistic-model dominance. To attempt to do so would be to ignore the fact that the nursing aides also differ greatly in their degree of interest in any type of service delivery at all. On the one hand, for a nursing aide who is above average in interest in service delivery, the question of medical-model dominance versus humanistic-model dominance becomes a salient one. On the other hand, for nursing aides who are well below average in interest in service delivery (who are just putting in their hours), the issue of medical-model dominance versus humanistic-model dominance is irrelevant. A social-climate questionnaire comparing these two models of service delivery might extract humanistic-model answers from nursing aides and other staff members who really have no interest in service delivery and would therefore

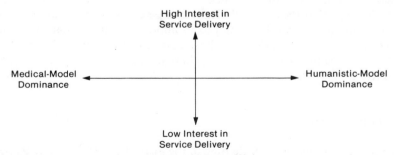

Figure 3-1. Service-Delivery Orientations of Staff in Institutions for the Aged

present a severely distorted view of the tone of the institution and the experiences of the individuals who reside within it.

Administrators

The administrator in an institution for the aged has the formal power to
dominate institutional life, but he or she often delegates this power to the
director of nursing, and this move effectively dooms the institution to a
high level of medical-model dominance unless the director of nursing is
unusually humanistic. The administrative category in a geriatric institution
includes receptionists, secretaries, the business manager, the personal director, the admissions director, the director of nursing, top-level nursing
supervisors, and any existing special assistants to the administrator. Not all
of these positions are filled by discrete individuals in every institution. The
functions indicated by these positions may be merged in the same individuals in small facilities, while each single function may be carried out by
more than one individual in very large facilities.

Table 3–2 shows that there are eight basic types of administrative
employees in geriatric institutions. These types are formed by the intersection of three dimensions: (1) level of involvement in the daily life of the
institution, (2) service-delivery orientation, and (3) technical competence.
Administrative employees who have a relatively high level of involvement in
the daily life of the institution have much greater potential for humanizing
the institution than those who are relatively isolated from the residents,
their social activities, and the daily grind of bed and body work. It appears,
from our survey of the literature as well as our field investigations, that
administrative employees often find the humanistic model of service delivery to be irrelevant to the performance of their daily tasks. Even highly
humanistic administrators may not have much of an effect on the lives of
the residents unless they are technically competent in the techniques of institutional administration. Keeping this in mind, we can see that of the eight
cells displayed in table 3–2, only those administrators found in cell A_5 are
really in a position to provide fully humanizing leadership in a geriatric
institution.

Consultants

Consultants usually spend little time in the institution. Psychologists, social
workers, podiatrists, and speech therapists, for example, have little power
over institutional life and therefore are of minimal consequence for the
humanization of geriatric institutions. The fact that some of these consul-

Table 3-2
Naturalistic Typology of Administrators and Their Assistants in Institutions for the Aged

Service-Delivery Orientation and Technical Competence	Level of Involvement in Daily Life of the Institution	
	High	Low
Medical model		
High technical competence	A_1	A_2
Low technical competence	A_3	A_4
Humanistic model		
High technical competence	A_5	A_6
Low technical competence	A_7	A_8

tants are humanistically oriented is therefore of little relevance. In contrast, the second group of consultants has great power over institutional life—namely, the physicians (including psychiatrists) who must sign the residents' care plans. They are unfortunately frequently dominated by the medical model and pay little attention to the humanistic needs of the residents. There is a tendency to view any therapies that are not aimed at some physical need as trivial. One physician, agreeing to recreation therapy for his patient said, "Put her in lots of groups. It will keep her busy." Nursing staffs who recognize that residents have more than purely medical needs often have considerable difficulty in manipulating the physicians into signing care orders that will allow these needs to be met under the guise of the medical model for the purpose of reimbursement as per Title XIX regulations.

Therapeutic Professionals and Technicians

Geriatric institutions also have a category of therapeutic professionals and technicians. These workers are usually housed in separate departments such as occupational therapy, physical therapy, recreational therapy, and perhaps social work. One might expect considerable differences to exist among these departments in terms of their position on the continuum of service delivery running from medical-model dominance to humanistic-model dominance. Our field research indicates that this is not the case, however. Humanizing programs and individuals with humanistic attitudes toward geriatric service delivery can be found in physical-therapy and occupational-therapy departments and may be absent from recreational-therapy and social-work departments. It appears that the (1) service-delivery-model preferences of the individuals in these departments, (2) political positions of the departments and the competition for scarce resources and staff positions within the institution, and (3) philosophy of the institution as developed and interpreted by administrators are much more-important determinants of the placement of a therapeutic-professional department on the medical-model-humanization continuum of service delivery than the profession or work tasks represented in the department.

Support Staff

The final staff category in geriatric institutions is support staff. These individuals are primarily differentiated by department, usually into maintenance, dining, and housekeeping. The dietitian is usually the only support staff person with professional status. Support staff members are usually thought of as contributing to the maintenance of the institution rather than providing direct services to the residents. They may be ignored in descriptions and evaluations of institutional life. The implication of this attitude toward support staff is that they could not possibly contribute anything to the lives of the residents other than the performance of physical-support work tasks.

A closer examination of institutional life suggests a very different view of the importance of these workers. In the institutions we examined, they had no allegiance to the medical model, and although they also did not see themselves as involved in humanistic service delivery, they related to the residents as whole persons, not as complexes of problems. Many support staff members, like a minority of the nursing aides, were fairly close to the residents in age, ranging from 50 to 70 years old. These staff members shared many of the values and physical problems of the residents, albeit at a lower level of severity. They usually performed tasks that the residents once performed for themselves at home, such as repairing windows, fixing meals, and dusting dressers. Much interaction occurred between residents and staff as the jobs were performed, with residents' frequently assuming the active role of advisor and commentator rather than the more-usual role of passive recipient of services. In some cases the staff even permitted the residents to help them as they performed these tasks. The sum total of these characteristics suggests that support staff can be a powerful humanizing influence on the lives of residents in institutions for the aged.

Residents

Residents cannot meaningfully be classified into as few cells of a property space as the various types of staff members. Table 3–3 presents a natural-

Table 3-3

Naturalistic Typology of Residents in Institutions for the Aged at Point of Admission

Social Background and Social Isolation	Health Status			
	High Physical, High Mental	Low Physical, High Mental	High Physical, Low Mental	Low Physical, Low Mental
White, middle class				
High social isolation	R_1	R_2	R_3	R_4
Low social isolation	R_5	R_6	R_7	R_8
White, lower class				
High social isolation	R_9	R_{10}	R_{11}	R_{12}
Low social isolation	R_{13}	R_{14}	R_{15}	R_{16}
Minority group				
High social isolation	R_{17}	R_{18}	R_{19}	R_{20}
Low social isolation	R_{21}	R_{22}	R_{23}	R_{24}

Note: Each resident group at the point of admission can be further classified, after a period of time in the institution, using the following adaptation types: (1) institutional withdrawal, (2) intransigent, (3) colonization, (4) conversion, (5) depression, and (6) nonreaction.

istic typology of residents at the point of admission to the institution. The cells in this table present the intersection of physical health, mental health, social background (which combines social class with minority-group status), and social isolation.

This two-by-two-by-three table is difficult to visualize since it compresses four dimensions into a two-dimensional property space. Residents are not equally distributed among the twenty-four cells in the table. High social isolation, white ethnicity, and low physical and mental health are more likely to be characteristic of residents in geriatric institutions than low social isolation, minority-group status, and high mental and physical health (Federal Council on the Aging 1981). We would therefore expect cells such as R_3, R_4, R_{11}, and R_{12} to be particularly heavily represented in most institutions for the aged.

Once the residents have been institutionalized, they can also be categorized in terms of their reactions to institutionalization. Goffman's (1961) typology of inmate adaptions to total institutions is relevant here. It consists of four dimensions:

1. *Situational withdrawal.* These residents substantially withdraw from institutional life and focus their attention on only those events that

occur in their immediate vicinity. Sometimes these residents express extreme territoriality by jealously guarding their particular spot or chair in a corridor or lounge. Milly, for example, would lash out angrily at anyone, resident or staff, who inadvertently sat in her chair.

2. *Intransigence.* These residents openly refuse to cooperate with staff members by verbally abusing them and perhaps by insisting that they do not belong in the institution. In spite of their advanced age, some of these residents can inflict physical damage on staff members when they catch them at unexpected times. John was one resident who took particular delight in vilifying black staff and would frequently strike out with his cane as a staff member came within his reach.

3. *Colonization.* Colonizing residents expect to be in the institution until they die and want to make the best possible use of their remaining time. They make themselves at home and depart from being model residents only when staff members insist on treating them like patients instead of like human beings. One resident stated

> I chose to come here, and this is my home. I'm going to make the best of it. Besides, they do so much for us here. Why should I sit around and groan like some of them [other residents] do? I just wish that some of those young aides had more respect for us older folks. They act like we don't know anything.

4. *Conversion.* Some residents convert to the staff image of themselves as patients rather than as fully human beings. They do their best to behave like good patients and become increasingly passive with the passing of time. Some even argue that they should not have to care for themselves as staff is being paid to do so. They are unlikely to improve in the nursing home since they come to enjoy being taken care of, and their adaptive skills atrophy over the years. Florence typifies this behavior. She refuses to care for herself, insisting, "I'm so sick. No one knows how bad I feel. You should be taking care of me, not making me do all those things. I'm a sick old woman."

Goffman's typology of inmate adaptations was intended for all total institutions but was developed on the basis of his observations in a mental hospital. In geriatric institutions and, most particularly, skilled-care nursing homes, we must add two additional types of resident adaptations:

5. *Severe, long-term depression.* The shock of relocation to the institution combines with a number of other shocks recently suffered by some residents (such as loss of home, occupational status, spouse or other loved ones, and financial security) to provoke a severe, long-term depresssive reaction that has many of the characteristics of situational withdrawal but that is different from that adaptation in its etiology and

in the severity of its symptoms. Sometimes this depression is expressed by silent withdrawal. Clara, for example, lost her husband, her health, and her home within the space of three months. She now refuses all therapy aimed at restoring use of her limbs paralyzed by a stroke. She sits in her room, staring silently at the wall. Others mask their depression through smilingly compliant behavior in which all real affect is suppressed. Stella never complains. Her vacuous smile is nearly always fixed in place, even in the most inappropriate situations.

6. *Nonreaction.* Some residents no longer have an organized personality system when they enter the institution or loose their mental faculties while institutionalized. They no longer react to institutionalization, or to anything at all, in an organized fashion. These are the residents who are awaiting a physical death but who have already suffered a social death. Every morning, Paul is wheeled to his usual spot by the corner of the nurses station. He is very nearly a fixture there. He talks to no one, and few talk to him. When they do, this talk consists of staff's calling some conventional greeting in his direction. He is usually ignored. Most of his day is spent dozing, crying and moaning, and systematically removing his clothing.

In summary, six major groups of social roles exist in institutions for the aged. These are administrators and their assistants, consultants, therapeutic professionals and technicians, nursing staff, support staff, and residents. For the convenience of the reader, the following list summarizes these types and the most important differentiating characteristics by which they are categorized into subtypes:

Administrators and their assistants, including receptionists, secretaries, the business manager, the personnel director, the admissions officer, the director of nursing, and top-level nursing supervisors. Primarily differentiated in terms of:
Level of involvement in the daily life of the institution,
Technical compentence,
Position of the medical-model/humanization continuum.

Consultants, who usually spend little time in the institution:
Those having great power over institutional life: physicians, psychiatrists;
Those having relatively little power over institutional life: psychologists, social workers, podiatrists, speech therapists, and so on.

Therapeutic professionals and technicians:
Usually housed in separate departments such as occupational therapy, physical therapy, recreational therapy, and perhaps social work;
Primarily differentiated in terms of their position on the medical-model/humanization continuum.

Nursing staff:
   Director of nursing and top-level nursing supervisors (see *Administrators*);
   Registered nurses:
      Career geriatric nurses,
      Nurses who have retreated from hospital work because of the pressure.
   Licensed practical nurses:
      Career geriatric LPNs,
      College students,
      Promoted nurses aides.
   Nursing aides:
      Motivated by values and money or by money alone,
      Social backgrounds include the poor, college students, and working-class housewives (some displaced, some temporary in order to earn money for specific needs).

Support staff, who are primarily differentiated by department, usually into maintenance, dining, and housekeeping. The dietitian is the only support staff person with professional status.

Residents, who can be classified by:
   Degree of social isolation at the time of entrance into the institution;
   Social background, particularly social class and ethnicity;
   Health status, both physical and mental, roughly measured by ambulation, continence, and alertness;
   Reaction to institutionalization, which can be categorized using Goffman's typology of inmate adaptations to total institutions:
      Situational withdrawal;
      Intransigence;
      Colonization;
      Conversion;
      Severe, long-term depression;
      Nonreaction, in which there is no organized personality remaining in the individual from which a reactive type might emerge.

Themes Characteristic of the Institutional Environment

Anyone who spends a great deal of time observing social interaction in an institution will notice that certain themes occur again and again in conversation. These themes are major anchoring points of the world views of the actors in institutional life. They are not important merely because they are heard so often but rather because they capture the essence of the character of life in the institutions. In the four geriatric institutions we studied, themes could not be categorized in terms of specific departments or resident types. The only significant differentiation among themes was by the caste line between staff and residents.

Staff Themes

Fourteen themes were identified in the social interaction of staff members. Three of these are positive, three combine positive and negative elements, and eight are primarily negative themes. The following paragraphs briefly explain these themes.

1. *"We care, but the rest of them don't."* This theme expresses the conflict that many staff members have between the negative public image of the nursing-home industry and their own personal experiences in the facility. They know they can care about the welfare of the residents and that many other staff members in their own facility also care. However, they tend to believe the negative image of the nursing-home industry that is constantly placed before their eyes in a popular press. Their pride is therefore limited to their own work and their institution rather than being attached to the profession as a whole.

2. *"We're a home, not a hospital."* This theme expresses the humanistic feelings of the staff. It indicates that the life of the institution is not merely limited to the provision of medical services. It is instead a comprehensive regime that includes both medical and humanistic elements. Many staff members place an extremely high value on the homelike aspects of the institution and would not wish to work in an environment that was less humanizing.

3. *"We're one big, happy family."* Staff members who express this theme are referring to two types of social solidarity. The first is among staff members themselves, and the second is staff-resident solidarity, which extends across the caste line. As with theme 2, this theme expresses a strong humanistic commitment to institutional life.

4. *"This is 'flakesville,' but we're going to shape this place up."* With this theme, we move from purely positive themes to themes that include both positive and negative elements. "Flakesville" refers to the common staff observation that a number of the residents are crazy. This word refers to some of the psychiatric patients accepted into the institution but also to those aged and developmentally disabled residents who consistently display bizarre behavior. The reference to shaping up the institution seems to refer primarily to increasing the level of medical services provided to the residents. It also has a component of increasing the degree of the control exerted over those residents exhibiting bizarre behavior.

5. *"Let's do something for these poor people."* Although this theme incorporates a positive element of service delivery, it also contains a negative, paternalistic element. The residents are portrayed as receivers, not doers. They are pitied rather than respected. This theme represents a charitable attitude in the worst possible sense of the term.

6. *"We're doing the best we can despite the state."* Staff members usually view state inspections and other communications with the state as harassment and as interferring with proper service delivery to the residents The state is not viewed as enhancing the service-delivery capabilities of staff members but is instead seen as undermining those capabilities through myriad rigid and silly regulations. These regulations are viewed as making working conditions in the institution much more difficult and as taking up so much time that the needs of the residents must often be ignored.

7. *"They have to learn that they're not running the show."* This and the remaining staff themes are primarily negative in tone. Theme 7 arises from the desire to promote efficiency in medical-model terms; the institution should run like a well-oiled machine, and the residents should passively cooperate in their own medical treatment. After all, it is for their own good. Staff members expressing this theme believe that the residents should, in essence, learn their place in the new social order, much like blacks during the Reconstruction in the Deep South.

8. *"Keep them busy."* It is a common belief among staff members that activity is beneficial to the residents, even if the activity is essentially meaningless. Busy residents do not make trouble, and they make a better adjustment to institutional life. Also, the presence of a high level of activity can be presented to the community and families as evidence of the superior quality of care in the home. Staff members expressing this theme show no awareness of the possibility that meaningless activity for its own sake could be experienced as dehumanizing by the residents.

9. *"Get it down on paper."* Because of the rigidity of documentation required by state regulations, it is necessary that all medically relevant resident activities (and quite a few that are irrelevant) be carefully recorded on paper. This theme translates into, "Charting comes first." That is to say, charting must be done, even if it is fictitious and even if it means neglecting the immediate needs of the residents.

10. *"These people are getting a lot of charity."* This is a more-negative version of theme 5. It expresses the belief of some staff members that residents are receiving charity rather than justice. Some staff members believe that the excellent treatment received by residents in the facility is partly deserved, while other staff members believe that it is not deserved at all.

11. *"Nobody appreciates us or understands our problems."* The nobody that staff members are referring to in this theme does not mean the residents but rather people outside the institution, particularly media representatives. The unremitting negative image of institutions for the aged in the

popular press is not balanced by stories of sacrifice and heroism in service delivery to the residents of outstanding facilities. This strong prejudice against nursing homes has been verbalized even in scientific meetings when we have indicated that life for some residents, and in some geriatric institutions, is actually better than it was before admission. This theme also expresses the conviction of staff members that outsiders, including most family members, do not understand how difficult it is to care for those residents who are abusive, uncooperative, or senile.

12. *"They wouldn't be here if they had lived right."* This very negative theme suggests that many of the residents in the institution would not be there had they properly saved their money for their old age or had they developed good family relations. The inference is that their present state is a result of some sort of moral failing instead of a deficiency in the larger society or just an objective consequence of changes in social structure. The translation of what we might term the social condition of the residents into moral terms is dehumanizing for those residents who overhear these comments being made and is the basis for theme 10.

13. *"These families really don't care or they wouldn't put their people here."* This theme demeans the families of the residents and makes unreasonable demands on them. It assumes that they have infinite resources for the care of their loved ones, and it also implies a negative evaluation of institutional life. Ample evidence exists to show that many families do care very much about the residents they have placed in institutions, but these examples are seen as exceptions by staff members expressing this theme. Their status as exceptions makes it possible to recognize them without changing the generalization.

14. *"There's so much to do."* Staff members in geriatric institutions are chronically overworked. There is always more work than can possibly be done, and the high turnover means that invariably some staff positions are left unfilled. Staff members sometimes find the enormity of the tasks confronting them to be overwhelming.

Resident Themes

A total of thirteen themes were identified as being characteristic of the residents in the institutions studied. Four of these themes are essentially positive, two contain mixed positive and negative elements, and seven are essentially negative. These themes are briefly characterized in the following paragraphs.

1. *"They do so much for us here."* This theme is expressed by residents who are playing the good-patient role. They recognize that they are currently receiving much better care than they would at home or that there is no possibility that they could be at home under any circumstances. They

are appreciative of the level of care they receive and understanding about the limitations of staff members. Some of them may hope that they will receive a higher level of services than other residents because of their expression of verbal appreciation of staff members.

2. *"I do more now than I've ever done."* An alternative expression of this theme is, "There's so much to do, I can't keep up with it all." Many residents were socially isolated prior to admission to the facility or were unable to participate in many activities because of their physical infirmities. Now, with their physical conditions improved, or at least with increased access to various activities, they feel that their activity schedules are extremely full. There seems to be a redefinition of what constitutes a full schedule that occurs as people age, and attendance at an hour's therapy session in the morning and a bingo game in the afternoon is defined as "almost more than I can handle" by many residents.

3. *"I have friends here."* The social worlds of many of the infirm elderly are greatly expanded when they are admitted to a geriatric institution. They make friends with their roommates, and they meet other residents with whom they have much in common as they participate in therapy groups, meals, and other institutional activities.

4. *"I could go to live with them if I wanted to, but I don't want to be a burden."* Residents expressing this theme are making the best of a difficult situation. They may prefer to be living with a relative, and the relative may have actually made an offer for them to do so, but they realize that things would not go well if they were to accept the offer. In other cases, this theme is a cover for strong feelings of rejection by relatives perceived by the residents as having been too quick to admit them to the institution.

5. *"It's something to do."* We now leave the predominantly positive themes for two themes that mix positive and negative elements. There is an element of despair in this theme for some residents seem to view the activities of the institution as not being particularly meaningful and as just passing the time from day to day. Conversely, a positive element exists in this theme in that it expresses a willingness on the part of the residents to become involved in the activities of the institution. In some cases it is evident that the residents enjoy the activities much more than they wish to admit, and "It's something to do" is a way of being what some adolescents would call "cool" and avoiding the expression of too much enthusiasm for institutional activities.

6. *"They'll be old too some day, and then they'll know."* This theme expresses the wisdom and experience of the elderly residents as they confront the infirmities of old age. It also reflects what many residents take to be the inability of younger people (particularly staff members) to understand what it is really like to be old, to suffer constant pain, to be separated from one's loved ones, and to be unable to live one's accustomed life-style.

7. *"It's a funny farm."* The remaining themes in this list are predominantly negative in tone. Theme 7 is expressed by those residents who see their institution as primarily a place for incompetents and "crazies." Residents who take this position talk to staff, but they have few social contacts among their peers since they feel that the other residents are below them. These are also the residents who feel particularly contaminated by being forced to live with people whom they see as exhibiting either bizarre or incompetent behavior.

8. *"If I only had a son, I wouldn't be here."* The son in this theme sometimes becomes a daughter or another nonexistent relative. Alternatively, the lack may be the resident's house or loss of some other important possession or personal faculty. The point of the theme is that the resident does not belong here and has come to be here only because of some fatal flaw or tragic event in his or her personal history. This theme is analogous to the sad tales described by Goffman (1961) on the basis of his observation of residents in a mental institution.

9. *"I don't know why anyone should go on living like this. I'm good for nothing."* Some residents do not accept their increasing physical infirmities and judge themselves negatively as a result. These individuals express despair over their perception that their physical condition will never substantially improve and that they will never again be able to perform economically productive tasks—that is, to be useful.

10. *"The food is garbage."* In nursing homes, as in all other total institutions, the food is a focal point of many conversations. Few residents wish to admit that the food is good or even adequate. They are much more likely to claim that it is garbage and to try to outdo each other in making up outrageous stories about the quality of the food, its sources, or the way in which it is served. These stories seem to be much the same in institutions that serve high-quality food as in institutions that serve food of minimal quality, which suggests that the food itself is not the cause of the stories.

11. *"They're stealing me blind."* It is not easy for some residents to give up direct supervision of their financial affairs. Others become increasingly confused about financial matters as they age, and their forgetfulness is often translated into imagined thefts of their money by staff members.

12. *"That's how they are."* This comment is commonly made by white residents about black nursing aides. From their viewpoint, the black aides are lazy, dishonest, or dumb. These perceptions are often communicated directly to the black aides in extremely abusive language. Disparaging remarks sometimes are heard about the youth, inexperience, and discourtesy of both white and black aides.

13. *"They're too busy."* This final resident theme echos staff theme 14 and reflects the reality of life in geriatric institutions. There are never enough staff members to take care of all the needs of the residents as de-

fined by the medical model, to say nothing of their more fully human needs or additional self-defined needs. The expression of this theme by the residents sometimes takes on a particularly bitter tone when it is used to express their feeling that staff members do not really care about them as persons.

It must be understood that individual residents and staff members cannot be rigidly classified in terms of one or more themes. They express different themes in different social settings. It is entirely possible for a staff member to express two completely contradictory themes within the space of a few minutes in response to two different sets of environmental stimuli. Therefore, we may say that the logic of the view on institutional life expressed in each theme is situation specific rather that person specific.

Although we have presented separate sets of themes for staff and residents, and although the staff-resident caste line is a major element in geriatric institutions, it is also true that common definitions of situations are constantly being negotiated across the caste line. These common definitions may be fleeting, or more-or-less permanent aspects of the social life of the institution. They emerge as a response to the shared lives and common problems that occur in institutional life or perhaps as an outgrowth of commonalities in the social backgrounds of staff members and residents. They can also occur as asides to the caste line because individuals live on many different levels at once. The strength of the caste line varies from institution to institution and can be broken in even the most rigid institutions that are dominated by the medical model. In these institutions, alliances across the caste line and common definitions of the situation are perceived as exceptions to the rule so that they do not undermine the vitality of the caste line as a way of organizing and segmenting institutional social life.

Institutions for the Aged Compared to Prisons

Many of the nation's aged are prisoners of their own infirmities, regardless of whether they live at home or in an institution. They may be confined to a wheelchair and lack the strength to wheel themselves. They may be so sensitive to cold or damp conditions that they only go out in sunny weather. They may no longer be able to drive their own cars, or in the case of many aged women, they never drove themselves anywhere because their now deceased husbands insisted on doing all the driving. Increasing forgetfulness and unfamiliarity with contemporary business practices designed to mislead consumers may make them wary of doing business on their own.

The elderly are often prisoners of another insidious condition that, in times of high inflation, may deteriorate more rapidly than physical health—that is, lack of financial well-being. Creeping poverty is common among the elderly who are on relatively fixed incomes. It limits their ability to continue to live their accustomed life-styles. Both inflation-induced creeping poverty and absolute poverty make it impossible to adjust to the many physical infirmities that require architectural modifications in the home, special support services for housekeeping and financial management, or moving to a more-suitable climate.

We should not confuse the imprisoning implication of physical infirmities and poverty with our analysis of institutions for the aged as compared to prisons. Many of the residents of these institutions would not be able to enjoy complete freedom and a high level of physical and mental well-being outside of the institutions due to their poverty and/or health problems. Despite these qualifications, it is apparent that many similarities exist between correctional institutions and institutions for the aged. A comparison of data from our present study of three nursing homes and a community-based residential facility with Bowker's (1980) observations in the Walla Walla State Penitentiary and other correctional institutions over the period of a decade suggests the following similarities.

1. Resident-staff social interaction tends to be restricted in both settings. A caste line rigidly separates staff from residents in all but the most humanistic institutions. In prisons, this caste line is supported by legal requirements for custody and the imputations of moral despicability to the characters of the prisoners. Neither of these factors is nearly as important in nursing homes, but they are supplemented by the medical model and translations of the mental infirmities and lack of independence of some nursing-home residents into moral terms. Like guards, nurses and aides supposedly know what is best for the residents, and this corpus of knowledge is couched in terms that usually take little account of the fully human (as opposed to the physical biological) needs of the residents.

2. Most nursing-home residents do not appear to leave their institutions any more often than prisoners leave correctional institutions. They are effectively imprisoned within the walls of their nursing homes by a combination of poverty, infirmities, and lack of institutional programs, personnel, and equipment designed to minimize institutional isolation. For example, lack of a trips director and a van with a wheelchair lift can effectively confine many residents to a facility. As in prisons, this physical isolation leads to emotional and social isolation from the larger society and to an intense focus upon life within the institution. Minor events become major topics of conversation and concern, and residents are particularly vulnerable to the social manipulations of their peers and staff members because they have lost the balancing perspective that is provided by the larger web of meaningful relationships that they may have experienced prior to institutionalization.

3. Role engulfment is a characteristic of resident and staff behavior in nursing homes as well as prisons. Zimbardo's (1972) pseudoprison experiment is paralleled by the pseudo-nursing-home experiment conducted by Wigdor, Nelson, and Hickerson (1977). In both cases, normal, noninstitu-

tionalized individuals playing the roles of staff members and residents shared, within hours, behavioral changes indicative of role engulfment. The social pressure to behave like a good patient/prisoner/resident or like a good nurse/aid/guard can be overwhelming in the pressure-cooker atmosphere of institutional life. To be sure, some residents resist this pressure, and the formal and informal sanctions applied to them because of their deviance serve to warn others that an iron fist is in the velvet glove. The abstract forms of staff and resident social behavior that Goffman (1961) created, based on his observations in a mental institution, have high applicability to behavior in both prisons and institutions for the aged.

4. The socially structured gulf between residents and staff members leaves residents feeling powerless to control their own living conditions. As a group, they react to this powerlessness by constantly griping about institutional conditions. It is either too hot or too cold; staff members are rough and unkind; and the food is always bad. A paranoia about staff's listening in on resident conversations led the wealthier residents in one institution for the aged to install their own external phones so the switchboard operator for the institution could not listen in on their calls. The dissatisfaction with institutional food is endemic no matter how varied and nutritionally sound the menu. Many bizarre stories make the rounds about food sources, food preparation, and food service, along with a great deal of gallows humor about it all. It is disconcerting to hear the same phrases being used to describe food by elderly women in an upper-middle-class institution for the aged that had been previously overheard being used by lower-class violence-prone prisoners in maximum-security prisons.

5. Considerable self-selection and social filtering occurs before residents enter either prisons or nursing homes. Prisoners are not a cross section of criminals, and nursing-home residents are not a cross section of the elderly. The filtering process that occurs in the criminal-justice system is well understood, but comparatively little is known about the paths by which prospective residents reach the doors of institutions for the aged. Aside from financial and health considerations, other selective processes evidently are at work. For example, the black aged are underrepresented in nursing homes (Schafft 1980), and evidence on the high level of social isolation before admission of nursing-home residents (Bennett and Nahemow 1965; Masciocchi, Poulshock, and Brody 1979) reinforces the commonsense understanding that social isolation is one of the factors in the decision to press for institutionalization.

6. These filtering processes lead to another similarity between prisons and institutions for the aged. The phenomenon of contamination is one of the major pains of imprisonment, and it is also a major problem in nursing-home life. In nursing homes, contamination arises for the alert residents in three ways: (1) contact with elderly residents who exhibit bizarre behavior

because of mental deterioration; (2) contact with younger psychiatric and the more severely developmentally disabled residents, which may imply to the alert elderly that they have been reduced to the status of psychiatric patients; and (3) contact with staff members who are from socioeconomic, ethnic, and religious groups with which the residents would not freely choose to associate. It is perfectly true that psychiatric and severely developmentally disabled residents may benefit from contact with normal residents, but few of the alert elderly residents are in a position to provide that contact without sustaining damage to their self-images. When the proportion of these residents in an institution begins to approach one-quarter, as it is in many U.S. nursing homes (Abdellah and Chow 1976), the character of life in these facilities is dramatically altered. Contamination for prisoners means having to live with dangerous peers. For many black prisoners, it also means being forced to be subservient to white guards who come from the group that the black prisoners label as oppressors. In nursing homes, the situation is often reversed, with white residents' being bathed, dressed, and fed by black nursing aides (Shore 1972–1973).

7. This brings us to the topic of victimization. There is considerable victimization among prisoners as well as among prisoners and guards. This victimization occurs at four levels: (1) physical (including sexual), (2) psychological, (3) economic, and (4) social. In institutions for the aged, a surprising amount of physical conflict exists among residents. Stealing is so common in many institutions that some residents take all their valuables with them when they leave their rooms, and there is a high level of verbal abuse (which constitutes psychological and social victimization). An alert and caring staff can minimize the physical and economic victimization that occurs among residents, but verbal abuse seems to be beyond control. Decreasing victimization often requires an increase in staff, which is fiscally impossible in most institutions, and it would also tend to increase institutional totality. Staff members as well as residents are the targets of this abuse, and it frequently affects their morale. Racial abuse directed toward black nursing aides by residents was endemic in several of the Milwaukee nursing homes that we studied.

8. Another major similarity between prisons and nursing homes is the nearly total absence of privacy and personal space. In prisons, this lack is evidenced by the constant presence of guards and other inmates. Even the most personal bodily functions are not performed privately. A like situation exists in nursing homes, because residents are nearly always under the surveillance of staff and other residents. In one facility, mirrors were even used by staff to monitor lounge areas. Few residents can afford private rooms, and few of these rooms exist in most facilities. Hence, no opportunity exists for the expression of sexuality. Neither, in these circumstances, is there much room for personal possessions. Although lip service is paid to the resi-

dents' right to privacy, doors and bed curtains often remain open during bathing, dressing, and other forms of intimate personal care. Visits in nursing homes are not deliberately monitored as they are in prisons, but few private areas are available to residents for visits. The effect of this lack of privacy and personal space in nursing homes is revealed in the extreme territoriality of many residents. This territoriality and craving for personal space frequently takes the form of residents' refusing to acknowledge the very presence of other residents in a nonhostile way (Tate 1980).

9. The character of institutional life in both prisons and institutions for the aged is more a product of internal political processes and mundane work requirements than of the officially stated purpose(s) of the institutions. Guards and nursing aides must complete their mundane work assignments each day, no matter what idealistic job descriptions say they should be doing. Prisoners who help guards get the count done correctly three times a day may be rewarded by being permitted to victimize their peers in a number of ways. Nursing aides who are instructed to permit certain residents to dress and bathe themselves may do the job for them anyway to save time, thus reducing instead of enhancing the independence of the residents. The conflict between the custody and treatment staffs in prisons is a prime determinant of the placement of the institution on the treatment-custody continuum. The analogous internal political process in nursing homes occurs between the nursing staff and service groups such as the departments of physical therapy, occupational therapy, and recreational therapy.

It is important not to take the parallels that we have drawn between prisons and institutions for the aged as a criticism of the nursing-home industry. This class of total institutions is continuously maligned in the popular press, with examples being used from the worst institutions to indict the industry as a whole. Our intent is to show that the total-institutions perspective does apply to institutions for the elderly and that considerable potential exists for the application of insights from one area of institutional studies (correctional) to another (long-term care). At the same time, we do not mean to imply that nursing homes are doomed to have prisonlike characteristics. Quite to the contrary, we believe that the realization of prison/nursing-home parallels represents the first stage in the process of restructuring institutions for the elderly to minimize their levels of institutional totality and to maximize their ability to support the human growth and development of their residents. Furthermore, our own research in Milwaukee has shown us that some geriatric institutions can effectively combat the negative effects of institutional totalism.

Note

1. This and subsequent quotes are either taken directly from field notes or reconstructed from these field notes. Sometimes, the single character

presented is a composite of several different people. All names are fictitious.

References

Abdellah, Faye G., and Chow, Rita K. "Long-Term Care Facility Improvement—A Nationwide Research Effort." *Journal of Long-Term Care Administration* 4 (1976):5–19.

Bennett, Ruth, and Nahemow, Lucille. "The Relations between Social Isolation, Socialization and Adjustment in Residents of a Home for the Aging." In *Mental Impairment in the Aging,* edited by M.P. Lawton, pp. 88–105. Philadelphia: Maurice Jacobs, 1965.

Bowker, Lee H. *Prison Victimization,* pp. vii–viii. New York: Elsevier North Holland, 1980.

Federal Council on the Aging. *The Need for Long Term Care: Information and Issues.* Washington, D.C.: Government Printing Office, 1981.

Goffman, Erving. *Asylums.* Garden City, N.Y. Doubleday, 1961.

Masciocchi, Carla; Poulshock, S.W.; and Brody, Stanley. "Impairment Levels of Ill Elderly: Institutional and Community Perspective." Paper presented at the annual meeting of the Gerontological Society, Washington, D.C., 1979.

Schafft, Gretchen. "Nursing Home Care and the Minority Elderly." *Journal of Long-Term Care Administration* 8 (1980):1–31.

Shore, Herbert. "The Current Social Revolution and Its Impact on Jewish Nursing Homes." *Journal of Long-Term Care Administration* 1 (1972–1973):21–26.

Tate, Juanita W. "The Need for Personal Space in Institutions for the Elderly." *Journal of Gerontological Nursing* 6 (1980):439–449.

Wigdor, Reubin M.; Nelson, Jack; and Hickerson, Elzie. "The Behavioral Comparison of a Real vs. Mock Nursing Home." *Gerontologist* 17, 5 part 2 (1977):133.

Zimbardo, Phillip G. "Pathology of Imprisonment." *Society* 9 (1972):4–8.

4 The Relationships among Medical-Model Dominance, Institutional Totality, and the Humanization Level of Residents

Institutional (or organizational) totality (as indexed by high regimentation, low permeability, the presence of mortifications such as contamination and staff gossip about residents' deficiencies, castelike interaction between residents and staff members, and the strictly bureaucratic organization of work tasks to reach institutional goals) was related to cost per resident per day and to the level of programmed social interaction in the four Milwaukee institutions for the aged that we studied. The excess income implied by a high cost per resident per day was not necessarily spent to increase the subjectively experienced quality of life of the residents. It was often eaten up by additional medical services. Moreover, the term *excess* is misleading for two reasons. First, institutions housing a more medically needy population will be constrained to have higher rates than institutions housing residents in need of skilled care, but much less than total, intensive around-the-clock services. Second, proprietary institutions often deliver the same services for lower costs than nonprofit institutions due to more-efficient administrative practices (Koetting 1980).

Programmed social interaction also turned out to be a misleading concept because it was possible to organize such programs so rigidly (for example, a highly structured remotivation-therapy program) that no diminution of institutional totality occurred. In addition, we found that unprogrammed social interaction with nursing aides and other staff members, as well as social-interaction programs offered as occupational or physical therapy, were usually more important in the lives of residents than rigidly programmed social interaction under the direction of recreational therapists and social workers. In short, the label affixed to a given program department was not a dependable indicator of the humanizing social-interaction content of the program.

A considerable amount of variation existed between organizations on the dimension of institutional totality, but this variation was primarily associated with a variable that was not used in the selection of the sample—that is, the degree to which the medical model of patient care on institutional life was imposed. If the nursing department is dominant in an

51

institution, and if the nurses strongly favor the medical model (as they fre-quently do), then institutional life is likely to be dominated by the medical model. Medical-model dominance means that the social life of the institu-tion and the private lives of the residents are rigidly organized to ease the achievement of medical goals. Although the field of medicine is not totally unaware of the non-biological-system needs of human beings, these needs tend to be seen as important because of their contribution to physical health rather than as important in their own right. Medical-model standards for nursing-home life are dominant in the industry, and an acquaintance with standards such as those in the *Accreditation Manual for Long Term Care Facilities* produced by the Joint Commission of Accreditation on Hospitals (1979) reveals how little attention the medical profession pays to the fully human needs of nursing-home residents.

The Accreditation Manual contains seventy-four pages of detailed standards for long-term-care facilities, of which two pages are devoted to patient/resident activities, four pages to patient/resident rights and respon-sibilities, and only a brief paragraph to spiritual services. The standards contained in these sections are not comprehensive, but they are consistent with a humanistic approach to long-term care. The problem is that they are handled much more superficially than the medical-model standards. For example, the job description for the patient-activities coordinator, who does not even have to be full-time, is extremely general, while the job de-scriptions for the medical director and the director of nursing are lengthy and detailed. The lack of attention to the details of humanistic services in the *Accreditation Manual* gives nursing-home administrators much more leeway in meeting (or, more importantly, failing to meet) the fully human needs of nursing-home residents and implies that these quality-of-life dimensions are of limited importance in nursing-home life.

The federal guidelines in use in the nursing homes we studied were released by the Health Care Financing Administration in 1979. They are completely dominated by the medical model and say little about the non-medical needs of nursing-home residents. Social needs are only to be met if they are medically related. Patient activities should be ''appropriate to the needs and interests of patients, designed to promote opportunities for engaging in normal pursuits, including religious activities of their choice, if any'' (1979, p. 85). Residents' activities must be approved by their attending physicians to assure that they are not in conflict with their medical-treat-ment plans. There is no section on residents' rights, nor is there any require-ment to meet the humanistic needs of residents that go beyond the problem orientation of the medical model.

The proposal published in the *Federal Register* by the Health Care Financing Administration in mid–1980 would, if implemented at some future date, represent a significant improvement over the existing regulations. The new regulations do not mention providing humanistic support for staff members, but they do include a section on staff development that is limited to training for service delivery. The assessment form for resident care includes eight categories of information, only one of which is relevant to the humanization model—namely, the psychosocial category ("outside contacts, frequency of visitors, use of free time, preinstitutional hobbies and interests, participation in activities, communication, orientation, behavior")(Health Care Financing Admin. 1980, p. 47377). Social services are to be consistent with the assessment form (and therefore humanistically inadequate). The proposed qualifications for the social-services director permit the hiring of individuals with as little as a two-year college degree, and the qualifications for the patient-activities director (still *patient* instead of *resident*) are even weaker. As a result, it is unlikely that the occupants of these positions will have a significant humanizing influence on institutional policies.

The strongest points in these proposed regulations, from the viewpoint of the humanistic model of nursing-home life, are the sections on furnishings and patients' rights. Furnishings must "promote a homelike atmosphere" and residents "must be permitted and encouraged to have personal possessions in their rooms that do not interfere with their care, treatment, or well-being or that of other patients" (p. 47382). The long section on the rights of residents is admirable in its treatment of notification, access, resident councils, privacy, and residents' involvement in their own care plans. However, certain details such as how privacy is to be maintained in double rooms; the size of print, location, and height of posted rights, policies, and procedures; and the ways in which residents are to be involved in the development of their own care plans are not spelled out, leaving loopholes through which the intent of the regulations can be legally subverted.

Nursing homes in Wisconsin are also subject to the provisions of Chapter H32 of the Wisconsin Administrative Code that specify standards for service delivery that have been developed by the Wisconsin Department of Health and Social Services (1980). Although still inadequate in terms of the humanistic model proposed in this book, Chapter H32 requires much more attention to the humanistic needs of nursing-home residents than the federal regulations currently in force, and it follows the humanistic model more closely on some dimensions than the proposed new federal regulations. Although the word *sexual* is not used, there is a requirement for privacy during visits by spouses that obviously has sexual connotations. (However, there is no similar requirement for nonspouse contacts such as in dating.) The strong Chapter H32 section on the rights of residents contrasts with rather weak sections on social services and patient activities. The social-services section recognizes only those psychosocial needs that are related to health as defined in the medical model. Social-service staff are to serve residents only "when medically related social problems are recognized [in order] to initiate action to resolve them" (pp. 104–123). The discussion of resident needs is almost completely in terms of problems, which implies a negative definition of the residents. There is no mention of human growth and development. It sometimes appears that framers of state and federal regulations do not know that residents actually live in nursing homes, that they do not just receive treatment and die there.

In our study, we found that the higher the dominance of medical-model ideology in an institution, the higher the institution's level of organizational totality. Partially a product of the internal politics of the institution, and obviously influenced by the service philosophy and administrative style of the institution's chief executive, and the need of families to legitimate the institutionalization of their loved ones in medical terms (Karcher and Linden 1974), the degree of medical-model dominance is also strongly affected by the medical needs of the residents. The poorer their health, the more their medical needs come to dominate institutional life and the more difficult and expensive it is to provide them with a high level of humanistically oriented activities that have direct relevance to the medical regimen of the institution. This relationship also has a built-in feedback mechanism because a high level of medical-model dominance combined with a weak emphasis on the fully human needs of residents tends to depress indicators of physical health still further as the lack of humanistic stimulation undermines the residents' willingness to fight to remain ambulatory, continent, and alert.

Evidently considerable conceptual overlap exists among the variables of medical-model dominance, institutional totality, and the humanization level of residents. To help to sort out the differences between these concepts, we have summarized our understanding of them in table 4–1. The humanization concept can be stated either positively (humanization) or negatively (dehumanization). It is stated negatively in this case to be consistent with the negative implications of medical-model dominance and institutional totality. However, the four basic dimensions and the thirty-three specific indexes (see chapter 5) that are drawn from the humanization/ dehumanization dimensions are the same whether the concept is stated positively or negatively.

We see medical-model dominance as having both cultural-system and social-system aspects. Such dominance is justified by ideological arguments about physical health, professionalism, and efficiency. This cultural justificatory apparatus complements the social-system basis for its operation through institutional practices. High medical-model dominance results in the residents' being seen as patients with problems rather than as fully human beings. Their problems are treated in isolation from each other rather than as integrated aspects of single, complex human beings. Resident

Table 4-1

Conceptual Housekeeping for Medical-Model Dominance, Institutional Totality, and Dehumanization as Applied in Institutions for the Aged

Medical-Model Dominance	Institutional Totality	Dehumanization of Residents
Primary System Levels		
Cultural (ideology) Social (institutional practices)	Social (institutional practices, staff-resident interaction)	Cultural Social Psychological Physical (architectural)
Indexes		
People seen as problems, not fully human—that is, patients, not residents	Regimentation of residents' activities	Structural design: 9 factors.
Problems treated in isolation, not holistically	Low institutional permeability	General administrative policies: 9 factors.
Nonmedical problems ignored or redefined in medical terms	Castelike interaction between staff and residents as well as among different staff groups	Programming: 8 factors.
Resident conditions must be redefined as problems in order to receive attention	Strictly bureaucratic organization of work tasks to reach institutional goals	Social relationships: 7 factors.
Reasons for institutionalization seen purely in medical terms	Mortification such as contamination and staff gossip about residents	

conditions that are not really problems come to be redefined as problems, or they receive no attention. Problems that are nonmedical in nature are often ignored or are frequently redefined in medical terms. It is hard for practitioners operating under the medical model to recognize the legitimacy of any nonmedical or partly medical reason for entering a geriatric institution.

Institutional totality, in contrast to the situation in a monastery or an army boot camp, does not have a fully developed cultural justification in geriatric institutions. All practitioners agree that it is something to be minimized as much as possible. It therefore exists primarily on the social-system level, consisting of institutional practices and manifesting itself in staff-resident interaction as well as interaction within the staff and resident groups. High institutional totality is indexed by factors such as the regimentation of the residents' activities; low permeability between the institution and the community; the maintenance of a caste line between staff and residents (as well as between staff members in nursing and those in the other departments); the rationalistic, bureaucratic organization of work tasks to reach institutional rather than personal goals; and the presence of resident mortifications such as being contaminated by forced contact with undesirable persons or conditions and suffering destructive staff gossip about themselves.

The dehumanization of residents also occurs primarily on the social-system level, but it has consequences and correlates on other system levels so table 4–1 also lists the cultural, psychological, and physical-environment levels as relevant to resident dehumanization. Resident dehumanization (or humanization) can be indexed by a number of elements of structural, environmental design; general administration policies for the operation of the institution; social, cultural, and spiritual programming; and the quality, quantity, and diversity of social relationships. These indexes are spelled out in some detail in chapter 5.

Truman Manor

Truman Manor avoided medical-model dominance by having no full-time medical staff members. As a community-based residential facility, it was free of the medical-staffing requirements of skilled- and intermediate-care facilities. A high degree of institutional totality could have existed despite the absence of the medical model. It did not, however, for a variety of reasons. First, there were few staff members of any kind, so their ability to control the lives of the residents was minimized. Second, many (but by no means all) of the residents were healthy enough to fend for themselves within the institution. Many of them were loners who had lived on the borderline of society all their lives, and they were fiercely individualistic. Finally, the urban location of the institution and its lack of restrictions on the movement of the residents resulted in a very high level of institutional permeability. Residents could stroll down to local bars for an afternoon drink or to nearby stores to pick up toiletries or other personal possessions. In doing so, they continued lifelong patterns of individual choice and competence.

In its outmoded architecture, inadequate staffing levels, questionable staff competence, and overall lack of attention to both the medical and the fully human needs of its residents, Truman Manor resembles the nursing-home industry as described in the muckraking literature. Yet the low level of institutional totality in Truman Manor permitted the residents to continue many of the habits they had practiced before entering the institution. The administration made few attempts to avoid institutional totality, but the residents slipped through the staff's fingers, so to speak, because of the low level of funding for institutional services. The lack of a humanizing counterforce in institutional policies is not crucial in producing a dehumanizing institution if the organization is too weak to impress its organizational philosophy on institutional life.

Hoover Home

There was no such escape for the residents at Hoover Home because the medical model was firmly in control. Generally competent and humane staff members, adequate nutrition, a clean and modern facility, and a number of social-activity programs made Hoover Home a model geriatric facility in many ways. Nursing aides scurried to complete their charted tasks on time, residents were kindly regimented in remotivation-therapy groups, and professional staff members were hopelessly enmeshed in the charting game. The charting game is a medical-model myth that purports to ensure that every resident gets needed care and that no resident gets more than is needed. This myth is perpetuated by Wisconsin's Chapter H32 nursing-home code and the Medicaid Title XIX reimbursement system. Resident conditions are defined in medical or quasi-medical terms, and goals for progress must be set to legitimate continued payments. Maintenance is not perceived as a goal that the state will accept for funding at Hoover Home and Roosevelt Residence, which means that resident conditions in these institutions must be defined as problems and residents must be defined as sick (that is, as patients). Since many resident conditions are not necessarily problems, since some resident problems relate to humanistic needs rather than medical needs, and since maintenance is the only realistic medical goal for some residents, the charting game reinforces the application of the medical model in inappropriate situations. It also forces nurses who wish to meet all of the needs of the residents to participate in an elaborate charade in which nonexistent problems are created to justify the receipt of needed services. Fictional progress toward inappropriate goals is recorded in order to assure continued funding for service delivery. In summary, no abuses were observed at Hoover Home, but the unchallenged dominance of the medical model apparently assured a high level of institutional totality that in turn was associated with a lower-than-optimum level of resident humanization.

Eisenhower Care Center

Eisenhower Care Center was also dominated by the medical model of nursing-home-service delivery. It had a slightly lower level of patient charges and fewer formal programs designed to foster social interaction than Hoover Home. Despite these disadvantages, institutional totality appeared to be lower at Eisenhower than at Hoover, and the humanization level of the residents was consequently higher. This was due to a number of factors that tended to weaken the link between medical-model dominance and institutional totality, including (1) the presence of many older staff members that reduced staff-resident social distance, (2) the heavy use of volunteers to supplement the very limited contingent of a full-time social worker and two part-time plus one full-time recreational-therapy staff members, (3) a religious ethic of service that was strongly humanistic, and (4) a nursing department that had been politically ineffectual until recent months. The high use of volunteers increased institutional permeability so that residents did not feel so isolated from the outside world. The staff-resident caste line was undermined because many staff members were old enough to share health problems and attitudes with the residents. The religious ethic of service had a similar effect and helped to produce affectionate relations of familylike intensity between staff and residents. The ineffectualness of nursing leadership in the past had allowed multiple definitions of resident needs to continue to exist in the institution so residents were not merely seen as complexes of clinical problems to be treated.

Roosevelt Residence

Medical services at Roosevelt Residence were in no way inferior to those offered at Hoover Home and Eisenhower Care Center. Where Roosevelt differed from Hoover and Eisenhower was that the medical needs of the residents were balanced against their humanistic needs in the competition for funds and staff positions between departments and in the attitudes and practices of administrators and staff members. Roosevelt showed us that a high level of medical services could be delivered to the institutionalized elderly without having the medical-model dominate institutional life. The administration at Roosevelt had declared an all-out war against medical-model dominance and institutional totality, with the result that residents were not dehumanized by being institutionalized. Quite to the contrary, many of them actually experienced higher levels of human development at Roosevelt than they had in the years prior to their admission to the institution. (This was also true of a smaller proportion of the residents at the other institutions studied.)

We do not summarize here the many humanizing programs found in Roosevelt Residence since they are discussed in detail as part of the humanizing suggestions in chapter 6. Instead, we focus on what appears to be the structural key to the political and therapeutic ascendency of humanization at Roosevelt. In prisons, wardens often hold themselves aloof from the daily affairs of the institution, turning de facto control of institutional life over to the associate superintendent for custody, who is the chief guard.

The parallel position—associate superintendent for treatment—is much less powerful, controlling only a few small (and usually inconsequential) programs and deferring to custody on all matters of any importance. The director of nursing in a nursing home is analogous to the associate superintendent for custody in a maximum-security prison, while the heads of recreational therapy, occupational therapy, and physical therapy are either relegated to the position of lieutenants under the director of nursing or given an independent, but impotent, status analogous to the position of associate superintendent for treatment in maximum-security prisons. This is why the internal politics of nursing homes usually result, as Austin and Kosberg (1976) have pointed out, in the dominance of resident life by the medical model.

Roosevelt Residence differs from the average nursing home (and from Hoover Home and Eisenhower Care Center) in that the director of recreation was promoted to a position that amounted to special assistant to the administrator, with wide influence over all areas of institutional life. Although this individual does not have formal authority over the director of nursing (just as the associate superintendent for custody does not have formal authority over the associate superintendent for treatment in maximum-security prisons), nursing defers to him or her where it is possible to do so without lowering the level of medical care in the facility. It is clear to everyone in the institution that this special assistant has the ear of the institution's administrator, and this gives him or her de facto authority over recreational therapy, physical therapy, occupational therapy, and other program and service areas.

In these brief descriptions of four Milwaukee-area geriatric institutions, we see how medical-model dominance translates into a high level of institutional totality, which in turn depresses the level of resident humanization. At the same time, we have illustrated two types of organizations in which this negative equation is not played out. In the first type, limited staffing and relatively low resident infirmity permit the residents largely to continue to live their own lives. In the second type, administrative determination to minimize the negative effects of institutional totality permits the delivery of high-quality medical services but blocks the generalization of the medical model into other areas of institutional life. This determination may be based either on a commitment to the principles of secular humanism or to a more formally religious view of human needs and human nature.

References

Austin, Michael J., and Kosberg, Jordan I. "Social Service Programming in Nursing Homes." *Health and Social Work* 1 (1976):40–55.

U.S. Health Care Financing Administration. *Interpretive Guidelines and Survey Procedures for Application of the Conditions of Participation for Skilled Nursing Facilities,* 20CFR Part 405. Washington, D.C.: Government Printing Office, 1979.

————. "Conditions of Participation for Skilled Nursing and Intermediate Care Facilities" (42CFR Parts 405, 442, and 483, Proposed Rule). *Federal Register* 45 (14 July 1980):47368–47285.

Joint Commission on Accreditation of Hospitals. *Accreditation Manual for Long Term Care Facilities.* Chicago, 1979.

Karcher, Charles J., and Linden, Leonard L. "Family Rejection of the Aging and Nursing Home Utilization." *International Journal of Aging and Human Development* 5 (1974): 231–244.

Koetting, Michael. *Nursing-Home Organization and Efficiency.* Lexington, Mass.: D.C. Health, 1980.

Wisconsin. Department of Health and Social Services. "Nursing Home Rules." Published as Chapter H32 of the Wisconsin Administrative Code, 1977, with additions in 1980.

5

The Humanization Causal Model

Thus far in this book we have surveyed the literature on humanization and dehumanization in geriatric institutions, briefly outlined our methodology, described the social roles and themes found in the institutions studied, demonstrated numerous parallels between nursing homes and maximum-security prisons (both of which are total institutions), developed a dehumanization equation, and shown how this equation applies in the four institutions we studied: Truman Manor, Hoover Home, Eisenhower Care Center, and Roosevelt Residence. One more task remains before moving on to consider ways of mitigating dehumanization and increasing the humanization of residents in geriatric institutions—that is, to outline our understanding of the relationships between the variables affecting the humanization level of residents in institutions for the aged and the variables that constitute the resident-humanization dimensions.

Table 5–1 summarizes our present understanding of the dimensions of humanization in institutions for the aged and their theoretical background. Three sets of variables constitute the theoretical background for the resident-humanization dimensions. These are the preconditions for humanization, enabling (or transitional) variables, and differentiating variables. The rationale for the preconditions of humanization follows from Maslow's (1968) need hierarchy. At one time, many of the basic survival needs of residents in institutions for the aged were unmet. Under these conditions, the residents paid little attention to their higher, more-humanistic, needs. With the advent of certification regulations and their accompanying inspections, the number of geriatric institutions in which the basic survival needs of the residents were not met declined precipitously. Only then did residents, administrators, and researchers begin to become concerned about humanization variables in nursing-home life.

Preconditions for Humanization

The preconditions for humanization are the conditions in the institutional setting that must be met before humanization needs can have a serious claim on institutional resources. In addition to biological-system maintenance

61

Table 5-1
A Preliminary Model of the Variables Affecting the Humanization Level of Residents in Institutions for the Aged

Preconditions for Humanization	Enabling (Transitional) Variables	Differentiating Variables	Resident-Humanization Variables
Biological-system maintenance such as medical, dietary, bed and body work	General cultural values favoring humanization	Social backgrounds of residents	Structural design modifications such as to provide adequate private space for residents, furniture design, and positioning
Staffing adequacy including stability, competence, functional completeness	Willingness to commit resources by family, administration, government	Functional health levels of residents, both physical and mental	General administrative policies including the promotion of resident councils and the degree of bureaucratic impersonality used in staff-resident communications and the minimizing of medical-model control over the lives of residents
Adequacy of facilities including sanitation, state of repair, design that facilitates resident mobility	Administrative policies to humanize staff	Financial Status of the institution	Programming such as the use of music, art, literature, religious, and other humanistic elements in programs and the development of humanizing rituals
Accessibility to community for community events and services, public transportation, visits by family and volunteers		Partially expressed as resident preferences	Social relationships including permanent staff assignments, low institutional permeability, and special in-service staff training in humanistic social relationships
Resident classification sufficient to meet treatment needs and to minimize victimization			

(the basic survival needs of the residents), adequate resident humanization is impossible without the preconditions of staffing adequacy, adequacy of facilities, resident classification, and accessibility to the community. Staffing adequacy refers to stability, competence, and functional completeness. A high turnover rate ensures that the institution will not be adequately staffed as does the hiring of incompetent workers or having a staff in which no personnel are available to perform certain functionally necessary tasks.

Residents are unlikely to experience high levels of humanization unless the facilities are in an adequate state of repair. They must also be designed to facilitate resident mobility, keeping in mind that many residents are confined to wheelchairs. In addition, proper sanitation must be practiced in the facility.

A completely isolated facility is unlikely to be experienced as humanized by its residents. It is important that the facility be accessible to the community so that residents can participate in community affairs and community people can easily enter the institution to participate in institutional activities. Accessibility is heightened if an institution is located in the city proper rather than the surrounding countryside. It is also useful to have easy access to public transportation such as bus routes and subways. Few residents are able to provide their own transportation, and some of their visitors may also be dependent on public transportation.

The final precondition for humanization that is shown in table 5-1 is resident classification. This precondition refers to the existence of a system for differentiating residents at the point of admission to the facility as well as during their lives in the institution so that they can be grouped with other residents who have similar needs and ability levels. For example, it is desirable to group the alert residents together so that they can interact more extensively than they would if scattered widely among the senile, developmentally disabled, and psychiatric residents. Proper resident classification fosters social interaction among the residents, efficiency in service delivery by staff members, and also minimizes the probability that the residents will be victimized by their peers. In particular, the housing of the frail elderly with young psychiatric residents and developmentally disabled residents invites the possibility of all kinds of victimization including burglary, robbery, assault, and (although much less frequently) rape.

Enabling Variables

Enabling variables are visualized as being transitional between the basic preconditions for humanization and the humanization process itself. Given the existence of the preconditions for humanization in an institution, the presence of the enabling variables is a major factor in permitting or encouraging humanization strategies to be carried out. For example, overall cultural values must favor the humanization of facilities for the aged, or the existence of the preconditions for humanization strategies will not lead to the implementation of these strategies. There must also be a willingness on the part of family members, institutional administrators, and governmental agencies to commit resources for the implementation of humanization strategies. In addition, staff members cannot be optimally humanizing in their relations with residents unless the administration is humanizing in its relations with the staff members. The chain of humanizing relationships extends from those with the greatest power in the institutional setting to those with the least power. Breaking the chain of influence at any point is bound to have negative effects on the humanization level of the residents. Staff members who are treated by administrators as machines for service delivery at minimum cost cannot possibly have great concern for the full range of resident-humanization needs that are to be met.

The preconditions for humanization are basically structural, or physical, in nature. In contrast, the enabling or transitional variables are basically cultural in nature. When we speak to individuals, we hear them express their attitudes and opinions. Although these are attributes of their personality systems, they also represent aspects of the cultural system that have been internalized by the individuals through the process of socialization. Cultural values and a more-specific willingness to commit resources to humanizing strategies depend upon an awareness of the fully human needs of the institutionalized elderly and the assigning of a high degree of importance to the meeting of those needs. It is entirely possible to assign geriatric facilities a high priority for funding but to conceive of that priority in purely medical terms so that little or no attention is paid to the more fully human needs of the residents in these facilities. In U.S. society, a great deal of support has been expressed for the well-being of the elderly, but little specific attention has been directed toward their humanistic needs. The medical resources that are currently devoted to long-term-care facilities are considerable. However, the relatively recent rise in the level of concern about quality of life and other ways of conceptualizing the humanization level of residents in geriatric facilities has not yet been fully institutionalized in terms of broad cultural values, funding priorities, and facility staffing patterns.

Differentiating Variables

Assuming that the preconditions for humanization are met and that the enabling variables are in place, we are in a position to consider the actual dimensions of resident humanization. Before this can occur, however, there is an additional complication. The differentiating variables of the social backgrounds of residents, the functional health levels of residents, and the financial status of the institution must be taken into account in deciding which humanization strategies can be developed. The notion of differentiating strategies was initially proposed by Kahana (1975) in her article, "Matching Environments to the Needs of the Aged: A Conceptual Scheme." In our conception, the idea of differentiating variables expresses the dictum that practically no humanization strategy exists that can be taken to be universal in its application.

The social backgrounds of residents are primarily social class (as measured by income, education, and occupation), religion, and ethnicity. On a more-idiosyncratic level, is the question of the pattern of social interaction in which each resident engaged before entering the institution and the meaning this interaction had for him or her. In Milwaukee, different class and ethnic groups view the same activity programs and social interaction with staff, peers, volunteers, and family members rather differently. Some groups value family interaction very highly and place a much lower value on social interaction with nonfamily members. In the Milwaukee geriatric institutions we studied, this appeared to be true of working-class groups of European origin. Middle-class residents who did not have a strong identification with a specific European ethnic group were more likely to be at home with nonfamily friendships and often defined even acquaintanceship-type contacts as significantly humanizing. Religion in the sense of adherence to doctrinal precepts was less important than social class and ethnicity in determining the humanization needs of the residents. For the most part, Catholic residents were quite happy to attend Protestant church services and to talk with Protestant chaplains, and Protestant residents found it meaningful to be involved in Catholic religious activities. The specific doctrines of a given religion appear to become less important to people as they become more physically infirm and confined to an institutional environment, but the essential value of religious experience does not diminish.

The physical and mental functional health levels of residents are less-slippery dimensions to work with than the residents' social backgrounds. Residents who are in poor physical health will share some humanization needs with residents who are in relatively good physical health (ambulatory and continent), but there will also be significant differences in their needs. As the mobility of a resident diminishes, the possibilities for trips outside of the institution also diminish. More resources must be brought to the individual if he or she is to continue to experience optimum human growth during this time of physical infirmity. Another aspect of the effect of physical health on humanization strategies is the obvious point that the rigor of the physical-activities program for an individual will have to decrease as physical health decreases. The same arguments can be made for functional mental health as for functional physical health. Humanizing programs need to be tailored to the alertness level of the individual, and many programs that are stimulating and growth enhancing for confused residents would be defined as insulting and demeaning by fully alert residents.

We have not attempted to provide a detailed guide for the operation of the health- and social-background-differentiating variables because most of the necessary information about these variables is coded in the residents' expressions of preferences for activity and other program participation. The best advice one can give to nursing-home administrators and other staff members is to listen to what the residents say they would find to be growth enhancing and then to provide those experiences for them to as great an extent as possible within the limitations of the facility and its budget.

This brings us to the third differentiating variable, a variable that signals a change in focus from the individual to the institution as the unit of analysis. By the financial status of the institution, we mean both ownership and level of funding. Proprietary institutions tend to be more efficient in service delivery than nonprofit institutions (Koetting 1980), which suggests that they can deliver a higher level of humanizing services per standard income than the nonprofit institutions, should they decide to do so. However, the profit motive may interfere with the use of income (which might otherwise become profit) to provide humanizing services to the residents. We did not observe this directly in our study, but we did see evidence that administrative inefficiency in a nonprofit facility could result in a lower level of resident humanization than would be the case in a proprietary institution that consistently showed a profit. It is also possible to argue that humanizing facilities can be more profitable than dehumanizing facilities because of increased community support, decreased problems with state inspectors, decreased staff turnover, and a public image that is positive enough to attract many private-pay residents (who are more profitable for corporations than Title XIX residents). A careful fiscal analysis of this proposition has not to our knowledge been carried out, nor are we prepared to do so at this point.

The second aspect of the financial status of a geriatric institution is cost per resident per day. Although it is usually true that higher cost per resident per day provides greater funds for humanizing activities (such as a bus with a wheelchair lift and a full-time chaplain), there is no reason to think that this will occur unless the differences in cost per resident per day are considerable. Otherwise, the differences may reflect no more than differences in the medical needs of the residents, the efficiency of the institution, its profit margin, or the proportion of private-pay residents.

Resident-Humanization Dimensions

Table 5–1 displays four groups of resident humanization dimensions: structural design, general administrative policies, programming, and social relationships. These are summary categories for thirty-three specific resident-humanization dimensions. Since we could not effectively display such a large number of dimensions in table 5-1, we presented them in a separate table. The remainder of this chapter consists of an explanation of each of the thirty-three dimensions displayed in table 5-2.

Structural Design

Structural design refers to more-or-less permanent aspects of the facility (such as walls, windows, and floor space), aspects of the physical environment that can be relatively easily modified (including the type of furniture used and its arrangement within the facility), and the use of living things, both plant and animal, to humanize physical structures. Three of the structural-design humanization dimensions refer to architectural design, the modification of which would entail major expenses for geriatric facilities. Dimensions 3, 4, and 6 are often deficient in geriatric institutions because so many of these institutions were built before the time when the residents' fully human needs were a major criterion for the design of congregate facilities. Residents do not always desire to be in the company of others. As a matter of fact, enforced company is experienced as contamination by many residents. The provision of adequate private space for residents is therefore important to the quality of life in the institution. Since the average nursing home in Milwaukee County houses less than 5 percent of its residents in private rooms, privacy is best accomplished by having a number of visiting rooms outside of the residents' private rooms and by having privacy screens or curtains that can be inserted between the beds in their own double bedrooms.

The lack of privacy in geriatric institutions affects an activity that has been of crucial importance in the lives of most residents: the expression of human sexuality. The elderly are not asexual; quite to the contrary, the expression of human sexuality is important to many elderly individuals although the frequency of their participation in sexual acts is likely to be lower than it was when they were younger. We are not speaking only of marital sexual relationships but also of the expression of physical affection between individuals who have lost their mates or who were never married (nursing-home dating) and autoeroticism. Imagine the degradation suffered by a nursing-home resident who has masturbated regularly for years, but who is no longer provided with the privacy to do so, and who suffers the censure of staff members for attempting to masturbate in the most private institutional area available.

Human interaction is affected by the environment in which it is carried out. Small, crowded, double bedrooms; long, poorly lit halls without furniture; and cavernous dayrooms do not represent the optimum environment

Table 5–2
Resident-Humanization Dimensions

Structural design
1. Space available for the keeping of personal possessions;
2. Use of color coding;
3. Provision of adequate private space for residents (including space for the expression of sexuality);
4. Provision of space for interaction among residents or between residents and other groups of people;
5. Use of bulletin boards and other information-giving devices;
6. Use of natural and artificial lighting;
7. Use of noninstitutional furniture;
8. Arrangement of furniture within private rooms and public spaces;
9. Use of living things to humanize physical structures.

General administrative policies
10. Facilitating family choice of an appropriate institution, alternate community services, and discharge;
11. Balancing borderline medical considerations with humanization needs;
12. Degree of bureaucratic impersonality used in communications between administrators and residents;
13. Degree of humanization of medical procedures, standards, and accounts;
14. Special focus on humanizing activities in the early months of each resident's institutionalization;
15. Promotion of personal responsibility and choice among residents, particularly in choosing whether to participate in programs sponsored by the institution;
16. Presence of flexibility of scheduling to meet the human needs of residents;
17. Support of resident councils and residents' rights and resident and family participation in treatment plans;
18. Use of triage in allotting time for the development of individualized treatment programs where total resources are limited.

Programming
19. Availability of humanistic counseling services;
20. Program opportunities for reminiscence;
21. Use of music, art, and other cultural achievements to humanize institutional life;
22. Inclusion of religious and other spiritual program elements;
23. Structuring programs specifically to achieve humanistic ends, including service to others, rather than to provide activity for its own sake;
24. Availability of family- and spouse-support groups;
25. Integration with the larger community encouraged by providing access, bringing in newspapers, having voting programs, and so on;
26. Defining and developing rituals for holidays, birthdays, and other potentially humanizing events.

Social relationships
27. Permanent assignments of staff members to specific areas in order to encourage humanistic staff-resident relationships;
28. Defining certain areas and times as particularly appropriate for informal staff-resident interaction;
29. Inclusion of people from the outside community in institutional events;
30. Recruitment and training of community volunteers;
31. Designation of special events for the joint participation of residents and their families (or surrogate families);
32. Encouragement of children and extended-family members to regularly visit the institution;
33. Training staff in humanistic social relations including the use of touch to communicate with the elderly and the social and psychological aspects of terminal care.

for social interaction. Halls could be designed with alcoves containing non-institutional furniture so that residents would be encouraged to stop and talk with each other and with visitors in informal, intimate settings. Large dayrooms are less useful than a series of smaller rooms into which residents and visitors can sort themselves for informal social interaction. There should be plenty of light without glare in geriatric facilities. Indirect fluorescent lighting can be used to supplement the inadequate design of windows where remodeling is beyond an institution's fiscal capability.

Given the limitations on funding, it is easier for geriatric institutions to make modifications on dimensions 1, 2, 5, 7, and 8 than to make major architectural modifications in the institution. Personal possessions are the physical reminders of the past lives of the residents. They are an aid to reminiscing, and they help to keep residents involved in the outside world. The more possessions a resident brings into the institution at the time of admission, the more humanizing his or her institutional experience will be. Institutions that make only a few drawers available for the personal possessions of residents are failing to meet their humanistic needs on dimension 1. Residents should be encouraged to bring a limited amount of furniture as well as a wide range of smaller personal possessions into the institution with them. They should be permitted to donate some furniture for use in the dayrooms and the halls of the facility. Personal places for valuables must be secure as theft is common in many geriatric facilities. A locked closet or other secure facility should be made available for each resident in the bedrooms, and more-valuable items such as jewelry should be kept in the institution's safe.

Drab coloration in geriatric institutions should be avoided at all costs. Variation in the use of color is stimulating and can also perform an orientation function if the colors are coded rather than randomly distributed. Even residents who are rather confused can learn to follow certain colors to their own rooms or to identify their rooms by unique decorations on their doors. Bulletin boards and other information-giving devices should be visible on the walls. They should be hung at wheelchair height and should be produced with print large enough to be read by residents with poor eyesight. The walls should also be adorned with cultural artifacts that have meaning to the residents, including paintings, drawings, photographs of resident activities, and plaques commemorating resident achievements. These cultural artifacts are also useful to confused residents as orienting devices.

Plenty of furniture should be available in the institution, and none of this furniture should have an institutional look to it (except for medical equipment that is unavoidably institutional at the present level of development. All furnishings must be functional in physical terms, but they should be as homelike as possible. The furniture in bedrooms and public spaces within the institution should be arranged so as to encourage rather than discourage social interaction. Isolated chairs spaced along a hall, or lined up along the walls in a dayroom, do not encourage social interaction. Chairs should be grouped together, with enough space between groups of chairs to suggest a certain amount of intimacy for social interaction. Chairs for visiting must be available in all resident bedrooms (unless residents request that they be removed), and extra chairs should be available to be brought to bedrooms when more than two visitors are present. The use of end tables in dayrooms may not be functional in physical terms, but it is an example of furnishings that remind the residents of home living instead of institutional living. Carpets are a desirable addition to the environment if they can be installed in such a way as to avoid retarding wheelchair travel. Shag area rugs with interesting designs in them are better hung on the walls as tapestries than scattered around dayrooms where they will make wheelchair travel exceedingly difficult. Rugs cannot be used in areas heavily frequented by incontinent residents, however.

A relatively inexpensive way to humanize an institution is to make extensive use of living things in the environment. Many different types of low-maintenance plants can be placed in the public areas of the institution, and these can be supplemented by the use of small animals within the limitations established by the interpretation of certification regulations. Birds, gerbils, and other animals in cages are easily controlled. Cats are perhaps the most humanizing animals of all, although they are difficult to control in an open institutional environment. It may be possible to make a few cats available to the residents in a part of the facility, such as a recreational-therapy area, that is shut off from the rest of the institution. Another possibility is to bring animals such as cats to a specific place within the institution during the day and to send them home with the staff members at night.

General Administrative Policies

The nine humanization dimensions listed under general administrative policies fall naturally into four groups. The first grouping is of policies relating to the admission of new residents. It consists of dimensions 10 and 14. It is important that administrators do not admit new residents simply to fill beds (a caution that is not needed in most urban institutions that have long waiting lists). Certain nursing-home applicants may be better off utilizing alternative community services or being discharged after only a short period of institutionalization. Even if long-term institutionalization is contemplated, nursing homes differ in their characteristics, with some being more appropriate for the needs of a given resident than others. Administrators and admissions counselors should communicate their humanistic concern for each resident who has applied for admission and also should be sensitive to the needs of the family members who are often undergoing considerable trauma as the result of the contemplated institutionalization of a loved one.

The newly institutionalized resident is likely to be suffering multiple traumata, not all of which may be apparent at the time of intake. In order to help the resident to overcome these traumata, a special focus on humanizing activities in the early months of each resident's institutionalization is desirable. This is quite the opposite of what happens in many institutions, where the residents gradually work their way into meaningful participation in institutional life over a period of time and are largely left to their own devices in the first weeks they spend in the institution. The initial assessment of the medical needs of the residents is paralleled by an initial assessment of their social and recreational needs (but not all of their humanistic needs). Program decisions aimed at meeting the full range of humanistic needs should be made at the time of the admissions conference. Some of the most important humanistic services to be made available to the resident can be provided by their peers rather than staff members through mechanisms such as a resident welcoming committee and a joint staff-resident orientation committee.

A second important area of general administrative policies is the interface between fiscal, medical, and humanistic considerations. This interface is addressed in dimensions 11, 13, and 18. Certification standards in Wisconsin already mandate balancing borderline medical considerations with humanization needs. For example, residents may not be restrained against their will when they are physically capable of walking just because staff members are legitimately afraid that they may injure themselves or that they may wander into a dangerous situation. Medical procedures do not have to dominate the lives of the residents although they may be dominated by their own infirmities if these physical problems are sufficiently severe. If the goal is to promote the total health and growth of the residents rather than merely their physical health, then there will naturally be many times when ideal medical procedures will have to be subordinated to humanistic concerns. This also applies to the rigidity of the scheduling of medication provision and the degree of resident involvement in the development of a medication plan.

There are no geriatric institutions known to this author that have adequate staff for the delivery of individualized treatment programs. Even the best staffed institution does not have enough staff members (assuming maximum voluntary assistance from the resident population where appropriate) to provide the full range of needed services to all residents at all times. In most institutions, the shortage of authorized positions in treatment programs and staff time in general to meet the individual needs of the residents is chronic and severe. The use of triage in allotting time for the development of individualized treatment programs is essential in these institutions. Unpleasant though it is to admit the reality of this situation, limited resources should be concentrated on those residents who can best make use of available programs and services within the parameters of existing certification standards for resident care.

A third area of general administrative policies is the area of the rights of residents, represented in dimensions 15 and 17. Nothing dehumanizes residents more quickly than taking away their freedom to choose what they want to do with their lives so long as they are well enough to have any control over their daily affairs. It is not appropriate to force residents to participate in programs against their will although it is acknowledged that some forms of gentle coercion are necessary in order to make the institution operate at all. Residents cannot make intelligent choices unless they are given full information about the range of choices available to them and the details of each choice. Using the philosophy of divide and conquer, administrators in total institutions sometimes attempt to isolate the residents, dealing with each of them on a one-to-one basis, which really pits each individual resident against the total power of the organization. This power imbalance is somewhat equalized in nursing homes by the creation and active support of a resident council that vigorously supports residents' rights and that takes an active role in institutional affairs through a series of subcommittees such as a food committee and an activities committee. Involving family members and residents, together with staff members, in the development of resident-care plans also ensures that a balanced perspective on these plans will be developed and that the rights and preferences of the residents will not be automatically subordinated to medical-model considerations of biological-system treatment.

The final area of administrative policies deal with the bureaucratization of institutional life and consists of dimensions 12 and 16. These two dimensions take the principles of administration-staff humanization, which constitute a precondition for the humanization of residents, and apply them to staff-resident and administration-resident interaction. The institution's administrators need to have personal contact with the residents on a regular basis and should make appearances at resident council meetings to discuss institutional problems with them. The bureaucratic impersonality implied by the posting of memo (single spaced, small print, and therefore unreadable for many residents) on a bulletin board without any resident input on the matter is inherently dehumanizing. Bureaucratic efficiency must be modified to include human concerns if institutions are to rate highly on these two dimensions.

Flexibility of scheduling is another area in which bureaucratic efficiency conflicts directly with human needs. Residents clearly cannot all arise whenever they want to and eat their meals at different times during the day. However, there is no reason why all of them have to be awakened every day of the year at an early hour and regimented in all of their daily activities. Again, suitable compromises should be worked out with the resident coun-

cil in each institution. Residents may be allowed to sleep in until 9:00 A.M.
on one or two days a week, even if that means missing breakfast. Other
schedule flexibilities can be built around visits from family members in
which they bring meals for residents, share institutional meals with them, or
otherwise participate in the activities of the institution.

Programming

The eight resident-humanization dimensions under the rubric of programming naturally fall into three groups. These are the cultural aspects of programming, the structuring of programs to achieve humanistic rather than
medical/therapeutic ends, and enhancing institutional permeability. This
third group of dimensions overlaps with dimensions from the fourth set of
dimensions on social relationships.

The cultural aspects of programming are treated in three dimensions:
21, 22, and 26. The first two of these three dimensions speak to the need
that all of us have to have our horizons broadened and our experiences
reinterpreted through acquaintance with humanistic materials ranging from
music and art through literature to philosophy and religion. Too many programs in nursing homes and other institutions for the aged amount to the
creation of structure without meaningful content; that is to say, what is important to staff members is often that the residents participate in so many
hours of this kind of therapy and so many hours of that kind of therapy,
administered according to to canons of the medical model, with little concern about the quality of the material that is used in the therapy sessions.
Reading material that sheds little insight into the human experience is considered to be just as beneficial as the classics of our civilization (which is not
to say that most residents should or would wish to read the classics). Reminiscing discussions are happily kept to the description of past activities
rather than to the discussion of their meaning for the residents. Practically
no attention is paid in some institutions to the provision of classes in philosophy, art, or music that are designed to reach humanistic goals. Music therapy, except when it is constricted by the medical-model view of residents as
patients, is a pleasant exception to this generalization.

Defining and developing rituals for holidays, birthdays, and other potentially humanizing events is not just a matter of structuring dates and
making arrangements for parties. The humanistic content of these events
can also be significant for the residents. It is one thing to have Christmas
celebrated in the facility and quite another thing to attempt to get the residents to think about the meaning of Christmas in their lives or in the lives of
others around them. Birthdays can become a celebration of life rather than
a celebration of cake and ice cream. Making special events into culturally

meaningful activities requires that residents be involved in planning them, that they be designed to have meaning that goes beyond the physical existence of the events themselves, that they be repeated on a regular and predictable basis (whether annually, monthly, or whatever), and that traditions be built up around each of these events to give them a depth of cultural meaning that extends beyond the temporal plane of experience.

The second group of programming humanization dimensions consists of dimensions 19, 20, and 23. A humanistic counseling service does not merely deal with problems in terms of clinical standards, and its goal is much more than to promote easy living within the facility. An easy-living counseling program sees residents who have problems that are defined in terms of the medical model. These problems, like medical illnesses, have temporarily lowered the level of health of the residents and often cause disruptions in the life of the institution. In practical terms, many of these residents have caused difficulties for staff members who are trying to complete their assigned tasks within the allotted time. In contrast, a humanistic counseling program focuses on what can be done to improve the situation of residents who may already be at a point of mental health, or equilibrium. The goal is not to restore their previous state of mental health but to enhance a sense of well-being and to promote personal growth toward what Maslow (1968) would describe as a state of self-actualization.

Reminiscence can be no more than a mechanical recalling of the activities of the past, or it can be handled more humanistically and be aimed at the integration of these reminiscences into a web of meaning that extends from the past to the present lives of the residents and that has implications for their future. The web of meaning is a key humanistic concept in geriatric institutional life as it is in life outside of institutional settings. Much of the aimlessness and depression observed in nursing homes arises not only because the residents are physically ill or feel abandoned but also because their lives have lost meaning. Therefore, a major goal of nursing-home life should be to restore meaning to those residents who have lost it and to help all residents to find new and increased meaning in life. This is what is meant by the admonition to structure programs specifically to achieve humanistic ends rather than simply to keep the residents busy by providing activities for their own sake or having goals that are limited to those recognized under the medical model.

Permeability is the key word for the final group of programming dimensions, and it consists of dimensions 24, and 25. It is difficult to avoid feeling abandoned if one is housed in a facility that has very low permeability. Few visitors and volunteers come into the facility, and the constantly blaring television sets are practically the only reminder that an outside world exists. Dimension 25 refers to bringing every conceivable positive aspect of the outer community into the institution. This dimension is heavily loaded on social relationships as well as programming and is reflected in dimensions 29 through 32 in the social-relationships section that follows shortly.

Family- and spouse-support programs meet a crucial need in nursing-home life. They deal with the guilt that family members have over placing a loved one in an institution and provide objective information about the services offered by the institution and the process of aging. At the same time, they bring family members into the institution more often than they might otherwise have come. The guilt experienced by family members is manifested in many strange ways including attacks upon the staff for not caring enough and finding themselves to be too busy to visit their institutionalized relatives. To the extent that family- and spouse-support groups can diminish the prevalence of these negative behaviors, they can increase the permeability of the facility and the humanization level of the residents in the facility and allow staff members to devote more time to productive service delivery.

Social Relationships

Institutionalization carries with it the risk of increased social isolation. Even if the isolation of the residents does not increase after admission to a geriatric facility, it is likely that many of them were quite isolated in the years before they entered the institution. Since the web of meaning is dependent upon immersion in social relationships, one of the impacts of social isolation is to make life less meaningful. Socially isolated residents are shut off from exposure to alternative definitions of their personal situations and of the world at large that might broaden their perspectives and help them to define their lives as meaningful and worthwhile. Because of these considerations we have structured one of the four groups of resident-humanization dimensions around the concept of social relationships. These dimensions fall into two natural groups. The first of these relates to increasing institutional permeability and consists of dimensions 29, 30, 31, and 32. Some residents may enter a geriatric institution to die in peace, but most of them hope to spend their remaining months or years as a participant in a meaningful community of human beings. Staff members, by their very nature, are forced to focus on the operation of the institution and the formal provision of services to the residents (many of these services being defined in terms of the medical model). Many of the residents are infirm and, being largely confined to the facility, need a significant flow of stimulation from outside the institutional social system as well as from staff and other residents in order to maximize their personal growth and sense of well-being. These four social-relationship dimensions visualize a facility in which non-staff members are constantly coming and going. Community volunteers come to be defined as honorary members of the geriatric institution and are invited to participate in many of the events that are traditionally limited to residents and staff members. Surrogate families are formed for residents who have no nearby family members of their own. These surrogate families may consist of volunteers, staff members, or other residents. In our field research, children were found to be a delight rather than a bother to the residents of nursing homes. In Roosevelt Residence, for instance, some of the volunteers were as young as twelve years old, and both the staff members and our own observations attested to the success of these young volunteers. Even younger children were regularly brought to Roosevelt Residence by families, staff members, and volunteers.

A second area of social relationships that needs more attention in most geriatric institutions is staff-resident social interaction. Dimensions 27, 28, and 33 refer to this topic. Institutions that constantly rotate staff members gain a certain efficiency in that staff members become acquainted with a wide range of tasks so they can fill in for each other when absenteeism or staff turnover occurs. Unfortunately, this limited gain in institutional efficiency is bought at a very high price in the loss of human contact between staff and residents. Staff who are permanently assigned to a group of residents become quasi-family members of that group. They come to know the health needs and personal preferences of the residents in much greater detail than can ever be learned from consulting residents' charts. The quality of their interaction with the residents is higher than the quality of interaction with rotating staff members because it contains a higher proportion of meaningful, humanistic expressions of affection and interchanges of opinions and feelings. It also gives staff a better understanding of the world views of the residents. These humanistic contacts make life more pleasureable and meaningful for the residents. They are interspersed with the performance of functional, medical-model tasks by the staff members in a continous, integrated flow of daily activities. Permanent staff assignment is a particularly effective technique when combined with special staff training in humanistic social relations including the use of touch to communicate with the residents.

It is also useful to define certain areas of the institution and certain times in the daily and weekly schedule as particularly appropriate for informal staff-resident interaction. This refers to interaction that goes beyond any medical model of direct service delivery. It simply means getting together in an informal setting in which residents and staff members can meet on an equal footing as friends rather than as providers and recipients of services. Nothing is more demeaning to the residents of a geriatric institution than to have staff constantly disappear during their breaks into lounges that residents are forbidden to enter by custom or regulation. This situation makes clear to the residents that they are seen by staff members as being no more than the recipients of service delivery instead of human beings to be valued on their own terms. A lounge area where staff can go to relax with other staff members and residents alike and that is defined as out of bounds to the traditional claims for service delivery is an example of what is referred to in dimension 28. Another possibility is to schedule resident and staff coffee hours together so that everyone who drops in for a cup of coffee will be on the same footing during that time. This is not to say that staff do not need a retreat available for their use at some times. To force them to be always in the presence of residents would be perceived as dehumanizing by many staff members.

Conclusions

The humanization model we have presented in this chapter is, like all models, an artificial construct. This material could be organized in many other ways. For example, some of the preconditions for humanization and the enabling variables could be folded into the resident-humanization dimensions so that only one list would cover everything that is now included in the four sequential groups of variables displayed in table 5-1.

A second point is that the material in this chapter should not be taken to be a final definition of the situation. Like other intellectual constructs, this conceptual model has a life of its own and will continue to be modified as additional information is added to our knowledge base and as our values change. We invite our readers to contribute to this process by sending us their comments regarding the modification of any of the dimensions included in the model, the addition of new dimensions to the model, and the reorganization of the structure of the model.

References

Kahana, Eva. "Matching Environments to the Needs of the Aged: A Conceptual Scheme." In *Late Life: Recent Developments in the Sociology of Aging,* edited by Jaber Gubrium, pp. 201–214. Springfield, Il.: Charles C Thomas, 1975.

Koetting, Michael. *Nursing-Home Organization and Efficiency.* Lexington, Mass.: Lexington Books, D.C. Heath and Company, 1980.

Maslow, Abraham H. *Toward a Psychology of Being.* Princeton, N.J.: Van Nostrand Reinhold, 1968.

6

Recommendations for Increasing Humanization in Geriatric Facilities

In this book we have suggested a causal chain running from medical-model dominance through institutional totality to resident dehumanization. (We realize that other factors contribute to this process, including institutional size, level of health care, the preinstitutional experiences of residents, efficiency of service delivery required by limited availability of funds, and state and federal certification regulations, but a full discussion of all these factors is beyond the scope of our investigation.) We have indicated the relationships between these three dimensions in each of the four institutions that we studied. Because the three nursing homes studied are all extremely fine institutions, our sample did not include any examples of institutions combining high institutional totality with low resident humanization, a combination that the muckracking literature suggests to be common in the nursing-home industry. For the reader's convenience, the study material is summarized in table 6–1. We now take a more-positive tack with a number of recommendations based on strategies that appeared to be successful in the humanization of residents in the four institutions participating in the project, plus those that our observations and a careful reading of the literature suggest as likely to be successful in enhancing resident humanization.

Most of these recommendations have already been implied in the literature summary (chapter 1), the dehumanization equation (chapter 4), and the humanization causal model (chapter 5). The recommendations in this chapter avoid the repetition of material from these chapters where possible. The thirty-three resident-humanization dimensions, the preconditions for humanization, the enabling variables, and the differentiating variables

Table 6–1
Relationships between Medical-Model Dominance, Institutional Totality, and Resident Humanization in Four Institutions for the Aged

Institution	Medical-Model Dominance	Institutional Totality	Resident Humanization
Hoover Home	High	High	Moderate
Truman Manor	Very low	Very low	Low
Roosevelt Residence	Moderately low	Low	Very high
Eisenhower Care Center	Moderately high	Moderately high	Moderately high

should all be taken as recommendations for the humanization of geriatric institutions. The reading of this chapter must be coupled with the reading of chapters 1, 4, and 5 in order to gain as full an understanding of humanization strategies in institutions for the aged as we are able to provide at this time.

Recommendations

1. It appears that humanization strategies in homes for the aged cannot hope to be effective unless the essential biological-system and physical-environment needs of the residents are met. In institutions or in individual situations where these needs are not being adequately met, the attention of the residents is focused on physical survival, and there is little energy remaining for the higher values of life.

2. Considerable evidence shows that the excessive mixing of residents with very different backgrounds and levels of functioning results in subjective feelings of contamination and dehumanization. A certain amount of mixing is healthy and stimulating, but too much mixing is counterproductive. Our observation is that an increased risk of victimization exists in nursing homes that have a high degree of mixing of residents from different backgrounds and residents with different levels of functional health. More specifically, victimization rates soar when younger developmentally disabled and mentally ill residents are added to the resident mix without adequate screening. Four types of victimization occur under these conditions: (1) physical (as in fighting), (2) psychological (deliberately provoking anxiety, being painfully insulting and so forth), (3) economic (theft), and (4) social (racial, ethnic, and religious discrimination).

3. State and federal regulations have been instrumental in raising the minimum level of physical and medical needs met in institutions for the aged. Paradoxically, there are numerous ways in which the implementation of these regulations has resulted in the dehumanization of residents. One of the ways in which this dehumanization occurs is that these regulations emphasize the medical model over a humanization model and thus direct the attention of staff members away from residents as individuals and toward residents as aggregations of specific clinical problems. The clinical-problem orientation followed by many professionals produces status distinctions, a lack of normal reciprocity, and inadequate communication of caring feelings between professionals and residents, all of which tend to decrease humanization. In Wisconsin, so much staff time is taken up in the keeping of treatment records and the performing of treatment-relevant tasks as per schedule that little time remains for informal, humanizing contacts between the residents and the staff members. Even worse, many humanizing goals

and activities are defined as nonreimbursable and therefore are given short shrift in the formal treatment plans required for every resident. State and federal nursing-home regulations need to be humanized and simplified to redirect the efforts of inspectors, nursing-home administrators, and staff members to a new focus on the comprehensive well-being of residents with a minimum of state regulatory interference in the process of service delivery. Institutions having an established record of superior care should not be given the same detailed inspections that are used to monitor new institutions and those institutions that past inspections have shown to provide an inferior level of care.

4. Residents can be encouraged to make choices about their own behavior and programming even when the outcomes of these choices may not be entirely in their best interest as defined in strictly medical terms by nursing staff. This strategy is a conscious abandonment of the we-know-what-is-best attitude, an attitude which is transferred from child care to elderly care in many institutions. Freedom of choice permits residents to casually rearrange their physical environments, converse with and assist one another, and go about their daily business without seeking staff approval or permission.

5. It is unrealistic to expect a high level of resident humanization unless there is a correspondingly high level of staff humanization. Staff members who feel dehumanized by the way in which they are handled by administrators are unlikely to be fully humanizing in their relationships with residents. Strategies for humanizing staff members include the accessibility of top-level administrators to all staff members as needed, staff support groups (to help them deal with abuse from residents, the stress of working with the dying, and other problems), the willingness of top-level administrators to perform any needed task in the facility (including changing beds and bathing residents) in the spirit of team work, the reinforcement of superior staff behavior through devices such as an employee of the month, the creation of structural mechanisms for the input of line staff members so that they know they are being listened to, and the development of a program of sports and recreational activities for staff members to help build staff solidarity.

6. The architectural design of facilities for the aging cannot easily be altered, but there are numerous relatively inexpensive ways in which the physical environment can be modified to make it more homelike instead of institutional in tone. For example, comfortable furniture, fish tanks, and other controlled environments for pets that are consistent with state and federal regulations, grandfather clocks, and many potted plants suggest a homelike atmosphere rather than an institutional setting. Small gathering areas permit resident interaction to occur with a modicum of privacy. Pictures of residents, family members, and staff members participating in humanizing activities such as trips, parties, and other social events can be

placed on the walls, along with plaques commemorating resident achievements, paintings, and other cultural items. The use of mirrors and variation in color and texture on wall and floor surfaces is also important (although floor textures should never be so rough as to impede wheelchair travel). Pictures, mirrors, and other wall objects should be hung at wheelchair height rather than standing height.

7. Residents should be encouraged to bring many personal possessions into the institution with them at the time of admission. These can include some pieces of furniture from the resident's previous places of residence as well as hobby materials, remembrances of past days, and other cultural artifacts. This policy permits residents' rooms to be as personalized and varied as possible, which also provides a means of establishing location for those residents who are temporarily or permanently confused.

8. Nursing-home services should be conceptualized as being delivered to entire family units rather than as service delivery only to individual residents. Family conferences, parties, regularly scheduled social events such as movies and bingo nights, and provisions for the regular sharing of meals between residents and family members are some of the ways of integrating family members into institutional life. Many family members could provide more-effective support to their relatives in nursing homes if they in turn received some support from nursing-home staff members. In particular, many family members would find it useful to participate in a support group with other family members in which they could work out their guilt feelings over having institutionalized their relatives and in which they might learn more about the problems and growth possibilities that are commonly found in nursing-home residents.

9. Institutional permeability can be further increased by the heavy use of volunteers. Volunteers can participate in nursing-home programs in many different ways. For example, some volunteers can provide direct services to residents, while others may do no more than to provide them with some humanizing interaction and continued contact with the outside world. The encouragement of children as volunteers, formally through the foster-grandparent program and informally as friendly visitors, is extremely humanizing in nursing-home environments.

10. Programs designed to minimize institutional isolation are not limited to those that simply bring outsiders into the institution. Also, many possibilities exist for involving nursing-home residents in community activities so long as their health permits it. Some residents are able to travel on their own and can ambulate or take buses and taxis to nearby stores, restaurants, and recreational facilities. Other residents can make similar trips with the help of staff members, family members, and volunteers. There is no reason to exclude residents from these activities just because they are confined to wheelchairs or because they have other infirmities. Attendance at

church services, cultural events, community celebrations, museums, and zoos are among the activities that have proved to be meaningful in nursing-home recreation programs.

11. It is not sufficient merely to provide humanizing services to residents. This approach still treats them as the passive recipients of the good will of others. A fully humanizing institution goes beyond this model of service delivery to stimulate residents to be truly active, innovative, and creative in their personal lives; political in their congregate activities; and to be the givers as well as the receivers of help and good will. Among the programs that fall under this category are resident councils, resident food committees, resident welcoming committees, resident radio stations, resident newspapers, resident operated stores and other businesses, charity projects run by residents for groups outside the institution, creative projects in all of the arts, and the provision for and encouragement of the expression of the full range of humanistic social relationships among residents, including sexual behavior.

12. Where possible, geriatric facilities should implement extensive day-care programs in which humanistic and medical services are provided to geriatric clients for four to twelve hours per day. These day-care programs would allow prospective nursing-home residents to remain in the community longer than they do at present, and it would also help to prepare them for the possibility of an eventual transfer of residence to the facility. This arrangement would have many advantages for the institution and the individuals involved. First, it would increase institutional permeability and help institutional residents to feel that they are still part of the larger community. Second, it would provide an alternate source of income, thereby increasing the fiscal stability of the institution. Third, it would greatly improve the image of the institution in the community. Fourth, it would make it easier to admit day clients to resident status because a complete clinical workup would already be available. Finally, it would decrease the trauma of institutionalization for the new residents and their family members, which in turn would reduce the demands that these adjustment phenomena currently make on staff time, energy, and emotional well-being.

13. One way to increase the chances that humanizing policies will be consistently followed in the institution and, in particular, that the medical model will not be allowed to dominate the more fully human needs of the residents is to create a new position in the staff hierarchy of the geriatric institution. This position would have a job description as detailed as the job description of the director of nursing and would have direct access to the institution's administrator at all times. The goal of the position would be to maximize the humanistic well-being (in contrast to the physical health) of the residents. Although the resident well-being coordinator, as we might title this position, would not have formal power over nursing activities, the

director of nursing would be constrained to give high priority to the humanistic aspects of nursing procedures by the informal power suggested by the close working relationship between this coordinator and the institution's administrator. In keeping with humanistic principles, it is best if the authority of the coordinator over other department heads be advisory with respect to day-to-day affairs, with formal sign-off authority being limited to new programs and annual plans for service delivery.

14. The trend of this book has been to recommend that the department of nursing lose political power within the institution on the assumption that it is a major source of medical-model indignities that are forced upon nursing-home residents. Although this is true in many institutions, it is unfair to think of nurses as being unconcerned with the more fully human needs of the residents. Many nurses are humanistically inclined and do the best they can to provide total care (instead of merely medical care) within the limitations of the certification regulations. The move to reduce the dominance of the department of nursing should be balanced by a program designed to convert nursing staff to a more-humanistic viewpoint through the efforts of a resident well-being coordinator and an extensive in-service training program.

It is obvious that successful strategies observed in specific settings will have to be replicated in many other settings before they can be judged to have the status of overall recommendations for nursing-home administration. As a matter of fact, it is likely that relatively few humanization strategies will be found to have universal application. Human interaction such as the demonstration of affection, sympathy, empathy, and general caring is probably always humanizing if it is without paternalism. However, specific activity programs and facility characteristics cannot be assumed to be humanizing for all the residents of an institution, or in all institutions, simply because they are judged to be humanizing by a researcher or an administrator. An activity program may be a humanizing influence on the life of one resident and an unwanted intrusion on the life of a second resident living in the same room. A series of such intrusions is likely to have a dehumanizing effect that is exacerbated if the resident feels pressured to participate in the activity against his or her will. Another complicating reality of institutional life is that the same activity takes on different meanings depending upon its institutional context. For example, a knitting class may become a symbol of alertness and high status among the residents in one institution, but it may be attended primarily by the less-alert residents and may therefore have a low-status reputation in a second institution. One may therefore say (following table 5-1) that some basic humanization strategies may be universal, but that others are differentiated by factors such as the social background and functional health levels of the residents. Furthermore, the success of these humanization strategies is dependent upon the institutional context in which the strategies are implemented.

Proposal for a Voluntary Humanization Audit

An apparent solution to the problem of dehumanization in geriatric facilities is to modify the certification regulations to eliminate requirements that tend to be dehumanizing and to add requirements that are humanizing for the residents. This ostensible solution is misleading for it is ultimately impossible to legislate humanization. Some changes in certification regulations will be most helpful, but the problem will not be satisfactorily solved through the regulation route. The regulations can assure that certain procedures are followed, certain services are offered, and certain rights are protected. They cannot require good will, positive affect in staff-resident interaction, and the extra effort by staff members that is always a characteristic of humanizing institutional environments. These elements of a fully humanized facility must be voluntarily adopted by the institution's administrators and given strong support by other administrative staff members so that they will be fully implemented at all levels of institutional life.

How can this be achieved if certification regulations, which have proved to be effective in raising the level of physical health care, are impotent to perform the same function for the more fully human needs of the residents? The answer is that we need to develop a humanization technology that can be approved by professional associations in the long-term-care industry and voluntarily adopted by corporations, boards of directors, and the administrators of individual geriatric institutions. We refer to this as a *humanization audit*.

The first step in developing a humanization audit is to precisely define the dimensions of resident humanization and those preconditions for humanization, enabling variables, and differentiating variables that are relevant to the implementation of humanization strategies in individual institutions. Chapter 5 represents a first step in this direction. Following the creation of precise definitions of humanization dimensions must be methods of measuring and evaluating the humanization dimensions and a specific set of strategies (practical guides) for increasing the humanization level on each of these dimensions. Elements of the practical guides for humanization strategies have been scattered throughout this book, but there has been no mention of measurement devices. The problem with measurement devices is that they force us to quantify what is essentially qualitative in nature. Keeping this fundamental deficiency of measurement in mind, we can make some projections about the forms these devices will take.

Measurement devices in the humanization audit will be of four basic types: (1) dichotomous items, (2) single-item, objective rating scales, (3) attitude or opinion items, and (4) multi-item scales. Dichotomous items record the presence or absence of a given element in the nursing-home environment. For example, are there family-support groups in the institution? Are chairs in common areas arranged in clusters so that residents face each other when sitting in them? Are chairs placed close enough to each other so that residents with mild hearing problems can easily interact? These dimensions can be rated in terms of either presence of absence rather than a more-complex rating scale.

The single-item, objective rating scale consists of three or more values arranged on a continuum from low humanization to high humanization. For example, to what extent is homelike furniture used in the residents' rooms? What is the number of program hours devoted to each category of humanizing-program activities? Most single-item rating scales will probably have five values, and an idealized description must be developed for each of the five values in every scale in order to be sure that the ratings are uniformly and accurately applied.

Attitude or opinion items differ from objective rating scales in that they focus on the subjective attitudes and opinions reported by residents, staff, and administrators instead of the auditors' ratings of specific, observable elements or practices in the facility. These attitude items will follow the Likert format (Babbie 1979), in which subjects react to a brief, simple attitude statement by checking one of five response categories: (1) strongly agree, (2) agree, (3) uncertain, (4) disagree, and (5) strongly disagree. Examples of attitude items that might be used in this format are, "Staff at this institution don't seem to care about me as a person"; "I find that I am more interested in life now than I was when I entered the institution"; and "I greatly enjoy the religious services that are conducted here in the home."

Multi-item scales compute scale values on the basis of responses to a number of separate attitude or observational items. These have been used in the past to measure life satisfaction, physical self-maintenance, minimal social behavior and morale (Lawton 1971); privacy, freedom, and integration (Pincus and Wood 1970); alienation and deprivation of freedom (Dudley and Hillery 1977); cohesion, independence, self-exploration, conflict, organization, resident influence, and physical comfort (Moos et al. 1979); and a number of other dimensions (Bloom 1975). Although many of these topics are closely related to our interest in humanization strategies, most of the scales are too long to be incorporated in a humanization audit that measures a large number of variables in a relatively short period of time. An additional problem is that most of the scales require a level of resident alertness that is not found in many of the institutionalized elderly. One of the requirements of a humanization audit is to have reliable and valid scales that contain a minimum number of items, perhaps following a Guttman rather than a Likert format, and to try to rely on humanistic interviews to obtain residents' opinions rather than to use highly technical and complex scales. [For a brief description of the Likert and Guttman scales, see Babbie (1979).]

Direct-observation rating scales, institutional records, and responses to a staff questionnaire will be relied upon to provide quantitative data from institutions in which the average alertness of the residents is relatively low as well as from institutions in which the average alertness of the residents is quite high. Although it would be possible for institutional administrators to purchase the humanization-audit manual that will be developed and to perform the audit in their own facilities, it would be preferable to have the audit performed by trained auditors who have completed a special course in humanization-audit techniques. The auditors could be administratively housed in a university unit, a state office, or a private corporation. It is expected that a trained auditor could complete an audit in a three- or four-day cycle, of which two days would be on-site. A humanization-audit unit, regardless of where it is organizationally situated, would need access to simple computer-processing services plus some secretarial and data-coding support. If the humanization audit could receive the endorsement of major long-term-care professional organizations, as well as other opinion leaders in the nursing-home industry, it could become an outstanding model for self-regulation in both the private and the nonprofit sectors of the health-care industry.

References

Babbie, Earl R. *The Practice of Social Research,* 2d ed. Belmont, Calif.: Wadsworth, 1979.

Bloom, Martin. "Evaluation Instruments: Tests and Measurements in Long-Term Care." In *Long-Term Care: A Handbook for Researchers, Planners, and Providers,* edited by S. Sherwood, pp. 573–638. New York: Spectrum, 1975.

Dudley, Charles J., and Hillery George A. "Freedom and Alienation in Homes for the Aged." *Gerontologist* 17 (1977):140–145.

Lawton, M. Powell. "The Functional Assessment of Elderly People." *Journal of the American Geriatrics Society* 19 (1971):465–481.

Moos, Rudolph H.; Gauvain, Mary; Lemke, Sonne; Max, Wendy; and Mehren, Barbara. "Assessing the Social Environments of Sheltered Care Settings." *Gerontologist* 19 (1979):74–82.

Pincus, Allen, and Wood, Vivian. "Methodological Issues in Measuring the Environment in Institutions for the Aged and Its Impact on Residents." *International Journal of Aging and Human Development* (1970):117–126.

Postscript

It is fair to say that the popular press has succeeded in thoroughly smearing the nursing-home industry by publicizing selected negative features, incidents, and institutions while largely ignoring the positive features and achievements of nursing homes and other institutions for the aged. These negativities are probably reported fairly accurately, and there is no reason to believe that they have been fabricated. The problem is that newspapers have not given as much space to descriptions and evaluations of positive nursing-home achievements as they have to negative revelations and scandals. (This is a subjective observation based on newspapers in the Milwaukee area. It would be interesting to quantify this subjective estimate using content analysis to examine articles on nursing homes in a national sample of newspapers.)

The one-sided treatment of the nursing-home industry in the popular press is echoed in the more-substantial analyses of the operation of nursing homes that have been published in book form. Surveying the monographic literature on the nursing-home industry, one is struck by the absence of positive material. There is much in the way of exposé and, more recently, a number of objective, statistical treatments of existing conditions but little in the way of a defense of the industry or a consideration of the positive potential of geriatric institutions in U.S. society. The scientific literature, as published in scholarly journals, is more neutral than negative, with only a scattering of positive articles. Most of the articles defending the industry or seriously examining its potential appear in periodicals such as *Nursing Homes* and the *Journal of Long-Term Care Administration,* which are serials with a small circulation limited almost entirely to the nursing-home industry itself. These publications therefore have almost no effect upon public opinion.

The essentially negative image of the nursing-home industry is paradoxically consistent with the needs of much of the U.S. public. Family members who feel guilty and inadequate over having institutionalized a loved one often want to strike out at someone in frustration. Criticisms of the nursing-home industry constitute an ideal opportunity for this expression of hostility. There is also an irrational rejection of the possibility of nursing-home institutionalization by many Americans who have not yet come to the point of making a decision about the institutionalization of a loved one. The logic seems to be that putting a family member in a nursing home is a terrible thing; therefore, nursing homes are terrible places. In addition, families sometimes blame institutions for their elderly relatives' natural deterioration.

89

The negative image of the nursing-home industry appears to have been internalized by many of the staff members in the four institutions we studied. This negative image is reflected in some of the staff themes that are examined in chapter 3. For example, many staff members (who should know better) glibly make negative statements about the inadequacies of families that have placed loved ones in a geriatric institution. The negative professional self-image of some staff members results in their being defensive about their work and ultimately results in a diminished quality of service delivery to institutional residents. In terms of our humanization model, we may say that the negativity of the image of the nursing-home industry is dehumanizing to nursing-home staff members and, through them, to nursing-home residents. To the extent that this negativity is undeserved by the industry, it is an unfortunate consequence of media policies and the psychological needs of some U.S. citizens.

We have seen many negative results of this destructive industry image in our research. However, the most negative possible adaptations were not found in the institutions we studied. Nursing-home staff members are analogous to police officers and correctional officers in the difficulty and stress of their work and also in the basically negative public image of their profession. Police officers and correctional officers have reacted to this situation by developing a rather narrow-minded clannishness. Officers in many police departments and correctional institutions are socially isolated from Americans outside of their professions, and the isolation extends to intellectual matters as well as social interaction. This has not yet occurred in geriatric long-term care, perhaps because it has so recently expanded into a major health-care industry.

It is unlikely that many public figures will emerge to defend nursing homes in the coming years. It would seem that the industry must rely on its own resources and become more active in defending itself. National long-term-care organizations need to take a more-aggressive stance in their public-relations operations and also need to devote funds to activities that will produce convincing documentation of the positive aspects of nursing-home life and increase our understanding of the potential for human development inherent in nursing-home living for the infirm elderly. One way this might be done is to begin a modest program of grants made available to industry experts and social scientists who wish to do research and to write position papers on innovative programs in nursing homes and ways of improving the quality of life in geriatric institutions.

Individual geriatric facilities lack the financial backing to hire in-house researchers and full-time public relations directors. However, each local unit of existing national long-term-care organizations could raise its membership fees considerably and pool the resources of area institutions to hire a full-time public-relations director who could see to it that the media were supplied with positive images of nursing-home life as well as the negative images that now captivate media presentations on the industry. Negative presentations will continue to occur as inadequate facilities are exposed (and hopefully reformed or closed). The intent of this suggestion is not to cover up these exposés but rather to balance the negative presentations with positive presentations so that the public will gain a more-rounded and fair view of the industry and its activities and so that nursing-home employees will have some of the burden of the present stigma of their work lifted from them.

Selected Bibliography on the Humanistic Needs of Nursing-Home Residents

Abrahams, J.P.; Wallach, H.F.; and Divens, S. "Behavioral Improvement in Long-Term Geriatric Patients during an Age-Integrated Psychosocial Rehabilitation Program." *Journal of the American Geriatric Society* 27 (1979):218–221.

Adams, E.B. *Reminiscence and Life Review in the Aged: A Guide for the Elderly, Their Families, Friends, and Service Providers.* Denton: Center for Studies in Aging, North Texas State University, 1979.

Adams, J.M. "Behavioral Contracting: An Effective Method of Intervention with the Elderly Nursing Home Patient." *Journal of Gerontological Social Work* 1 (1979):235–250.

Adler, S., and Carrara, B.S. "The Therapeutic Impact of Listening." In *Proceedings of the First North American Symposium on Long-Term Care Administration,* edited by American College of Nursing Home Administrators, pp. 23–27. Washington, D.C. 1975.

Alders, W. "The Idea of a Home for the Aged: A Re-appraisal." *Journal of the American Geriatrics Society* 9 (1961):943–946.

Altieri, A.J.; Sedutto, M.E.; Feder, H.M.; and Weissman, M.S. "Developing Quality Long-Term Care." *Geriatrics* 32 (1977):126–139.

Alvermann, M.M. "Toward Improving Geriatric Care with Environmental Intervention Emphasizing a Homelike Atmosphere: An Environmental Experience." *Journal of Gerontological Nursing* 5 (1979a):13–17.

———. "Toward Reducing Stress in the Institutionalized Elderly—Therapeutic Tape Recordings." *Journal of Gerontological Nursing* 5 (1979b): 21–26.

Anderson, N.N. "Institutionalization, Interaction, and Self-Conception in Aging." In *Older People and Their Social World,* edited by A.M. Rose and W.A. Peterson, pp. 245–257. Philadelphia: F.A. Davis, 1965.

———. "Approaches to Improving the Quality of Long-Term Care for Older Persons." *Gerontologist* 14 (1974):519–524.

Austin, M.J., and Kosberg, J.I. "Social Service Programming in Nursing Homes." *Health and Social Work* 1 (1976):40–55.

Bakdash, D.P. "Communicating with the Aged Parent: A System View." Journal of Gerontological Nursing 3 (1977):29–32.

Baltz, T.M., and Turner, G. "Development and Analysis of a Nursing Home Aide-Screening Device." *Gerontologist* 17 (1977):66–69.

Barney, J.L. "The Prerogative of Choice in Long-Term Care." *Gerontologist* 17 (1977):309–314.

Barns, E.K., and Shore, H.H. *Holiday Programming for Long-Term Care Facilities.* Denton: Center for Studies in Aging, North Texas State University, 1977.

Barry, J.T., and Miller, D.B. "The Nursing Home Visitor: Who, When, Where and for How Long?" *Long Term Care and Health Services Administration Quarterly* 4 (1980):261–274.

Beaudry, M.L. "Emotional and Psychological Support for Health Care Personnel." In *Proceedings of the Fourth North American Symposium on Long-Term Care Administration,* edited by American College of Nursing Home Administrators, pp. 17–26. Washington, D.C., 1979.

Beld, D.J. "Political Action Meeting in a Nursing Home." *Journal of Long-Term Care Administration* 1 (1972–1973):18–20.

Bennett, C. *Nursing Home Life: What It Is and What It Could Be.* New York: Tiresias Press, 1980.

Bennett, R. "The Meaning of Institutional Life." *Gerontologist* 3 (1963): 117–125.

Bennett, R., and Eisdorfer, C. "The Institutional Environment and Behavior Change." In *Long-Term Care: A Handbook for Researchers, Planners and Providers,* edited by S. Sherwood, pp. 391–453. New York: Spectrum Publications. 1975.

Bennett, R., and Nahemow, L. "Institutional Totality and Criteria of Social Adjustment in Residencies for the Aged." *Journal of Social Issues* 21 (1965):44–78.

———. "The Relations between Social Isolation, Socialization and Adjustment in Residents of a Home for the Aged." In *Mental Impairment in the Aged,* edited by M.P. Lawton and F.G. Lawton, pp. 88–105. Philadelphia: Philadelphia Geriatric Center, 1965.

Berdes, C. *Social Services for the Aged, Dying and Bereaved in International Perspective.* Washington, D.C.: International Federation on Aging, 1978.

Berezin, M.A. "The Psychiatrist and the Geriatric Patient: Partial Grief in Family Members and Others Who Care for the Elderly Patient." *Journal of Geriatric Psychiatry* 4 (1970):53–64.

Berger, R.M., and Rose, F.D. "Interpersonal Skills Training with Institutionalized Elderly Patients." *Journal of Gerontology* 32 (1977):346–353.

Bergman, S. *A Cross-National Perspective on Gerontology: Lectures by Simon Bergman.* Denton: Center for Studies in Aging, North Texas State University, 1979.

Berkman, B.G. "Mental Health and the Aging: A Review of the Literature for Clinical Social Workers." *Clinical Social Work Journal* 6 (1978): 230–245.

Berkman, B.G. and Rehr, H. "Social Needs of the Hospitalized Elderly: A Classification." *Social Work* 17 (1972):80–88.

Beverley, E.V. "Helping Your Patient Choose and Adjust to a Nursing Home." *Geriatrics* 31 (1976):115–126.

Blackman, D.K.; Howe, M.; and Pinkston, E.M. "Increasing Participation in Social Interaction of the Institutionalized Elderly." *Gerontologist* 16 (1976):69–76.

Blenkner, M. "The Place of the Nursing Home among Community Resources." *Journal of Geriatric Psychiatry* 1 (1968):135–150.

Bok, M. "Some Problems Milieu Treatment of the Chronic Older Mental Patients." *Gerontologist* 11 (1971):141–147.

Bourestom, N., and Tars, S. "Alterations in Life Patterns Following Nursing Home Relocation." *Gerontologist* 14 (1974):506–510.

Bowersox, J.L. "Architectural and Interior Design." In *Long Term Care of the Aging: A Socially Responsible Approach,* edited by L.J. Wasser, pp. 37–48. Washington, D.C.: American Association of Homes for the Aging, 1979.

Bowker, L.H., and Dinan, J. "The Assessment of Humanistic Needs in Nursing Homes and Other Institutions for the Aged." Paper presented at the Third National Conference on Needs Assessment in Health and Human Service Systems, Lexington, Kentucky, 1981a.

———. "Humanization and Organizational Totality in Institutions for the Aged." Paper presented at the annual meeting of the Society for the Study of Social Problems, Toronto, 1981b.

Brickel, C.M. "The Therapeutic Roles of Cat Mascots with a Hospital-Based Geriatric Population: A Staff Survey." *Gerontologist* 19 (1979): 368–372.

Brody, E.M. "Congregate Care Facilities and Mental Health of the Elderly." *International Journal of Aging and Human Development* 1 (1970):279–321.

———. *Long-Term Care of Older People: A Practical Guide.* New York: Human Sciences Press, 1977.

———. "Long-Term Care of the Aged: Promises and Prospects." *Health and Social Work* 4 (1979):30–59.

Brody, E.M., and Brody, S.J. "Decade of Decision for the Elderly." *Social Work* 19 (1974):544–554.

Brody, E.M., and Gottesman, L. "Issues of Institutional Care." In *A Social Work Guide for Long-Term Care Facilities,* edited by Brody, pp. 197–205. Washington, D.C.: Government Printing Office, 1974.

Brody, S.J., and Masciocchi, C.F. "Data for Long-Term Care Planning by

Health Systems Agencies." *American Journal of Public Health* 70 (1980):1194–1198.

Brody, S.J.; Poulshock, F.W.; and Masciocchi, C.F. "The Family Caring Unit: A Major Consideration in the Long-Term Support System." *Gerontologist* 18 (1978):556–561.

Cape, R.D.T.; Shorrock, C.; Tree, R.; Pablo, R.; Campbell, A.J.; and Seymour, D.G. "Square Pegs in Round Holes: A Study of Residents in Long-Term Institutions in London, Ont." *Canadian Medical Association Journal* 117 (1977):1284–1287.

Chappell, N.L., and Penning, M.J. "The Trend Away from Institutionalization: Humanism or Economic Efficiency?" *Research on Aging* 1 (1979):361–387.

Clarke, T.R. "Communicating with Residents and Their Families." In *Proceedings of the Fifth North American Symposium on Long-Term Care Administration,* edited by American College of Nursing Home Administrators, pp. 11–17. Washington, D.C., 1980.

Clarke, T.R., and Wallace, C. "Nursing Care Plans: Paper Compliance or Viable Plans." *Nursing Homes* 28 (1979):6–9.

Coe, R.M. "Self-Conception and Institutionalization." In *Older People and Their Social World,* edited by A.M. Rose and D.A. Peterson, pp. 228–257. Philadelphia: F.A. Davis, 1965.

Coffman, F.L. "Empathic Understanding: An Important Skill for Those Who Work with Older Adults." *Long Term Care and Health Services Administration Quarterly* 4 (1980):315–319.

Cohen, E.F. "Civil Liberties and the Frail Elderly." *Society* 15 (1978): 34–42.

Coons, D.H.; Gottesman, L.E.; and Donahue, W. *A Therapeutic Milieu for Geriatric Patients.* Ann Arbor: Division of Gerontology, University of Michigan, 1969.

Corbett, S.L. "Self-Concepts and Engagement in Society: A Study of Black Institutionalized Aged." Paper presented at the North Central Sociological Association Meeting, 1978.

Cornbleth, T., and Cornbleth, C. "Evaluation of the Effectiveness of Reality Orientation Classes in a Nursing Home Unit." *Journal of the American Geriatrics Society* 27 (1979):522–524.

Curry, T.J., and Ratliff, B.W. "The Effects of Nursing Home Size on Resident Isolation and Life Satisfaction." *Gerontologist* 13 (1973):295–298.

Daley, R.M., and Jost, D.T. "The Nursing Home Reform Act of 1979." *Illinois Bar Journal* 68 (1980):448–454.

De Long, A.J. "The Micro-Spatial Structure of the Older Person: Some Implications of Planning the Social and Spatial Environment." In *Spatial Behavior of Older People,* edited by L.A. Pastalan and D.H.

Carson, pp. 68–87. Ann Arbor, Mich.: Wayne State Institute of Gerontology, 1970.

DiBerardinis, J., and Gitlin, D. "A Holistic Assessment Model for Identifying Quality Care Indicators in Long Term Care." *Long Term Care and Health Services Administration Quarterly* 4 (1980):227–235.

Dick, H.R. and Friedsam, H.J. "Adjustments of Residents of Two Homes for the Aged." *Social Problems* 11 (1964):282–290.

Dickstein, H.W. "Family Guilt—A Study of Causes and Approaches." In *Proceedings of the Fourth North American Symposium on Long-Term Care Administration,* edited by the American College of Nursing Home Administrators, pp. 44–52. Washington, D.C., 1979.

Dobrof, R.; Metsch, J.M.; Moody, H.R.; Chalmers, T.C.; and Mathai-Davis, P. "The Long-Term Care Challenge: Rationalizing a Continuum of Care for Chronically Impaired Elderly." *Mount Sinai Journal of Medicine* 47 (1980):87–95.

Dooghe, G., and Venderleyden, L. "Social Adjustment of the Elderly Residing in Institutional Homes: A Multivariate Analysis." *International Journal of Aging and Human Development* 11 (1980):163–176.

Douglas, J.; Gaston, J.; and Wilkinson, W. "Nursing Home Aides: Who Are They and Why Are They There?" In *Proceedings of the Fourth North American Symposium on Long-Term Care Administration,* edited by American College of Nursing Home Administrators, pp. 53–66. Washington, D.C., 1979.

Driver, J. "Factors in Nursing Home Settings that Effect the Psychological Well-Being of Residents." *Long-Term Care and Health Services Administration Quarterly* 3 (1979):325–331.

Dudley, C.J., and Hillery, G.A. "Freedom and Alienation in Homes for the Aged." *Gerontologist* 17 (1977):140–145.

Dunlop, B.D. "Need for and Utilization of Long-Term Care among Elderly Americans." *Journal of Chronic Disease* 29 (1976):75–87.

Edwards, K.A. "Dining Experiences in the Institutionalized Setting." *Nursing Homes* 28 (1979):6–17.

Estes, C.L. *The Aging Enterprise.* San Francisco: Jossey-Bass, 1979.

Euster, G.L. "A System of Groups in Institutions for the Aged." *Social Casework* 52 (1971):523–529.

———. "Humanizing Institutional Environments for the Elderly: Some Social Interactional Perspectives." *Arete* 5 (1978):1–10.

Falk, U.A., and Falk, G. *The Nursing Home Dilemma.* San Francisco: R & E Research Associates, 1976.

Fallot, R.D. "The Impact on Mood of Verbal Reminiscing in Later Adulthood." *International Journal of Aging and Human Development* 10 (1979–1980):385–399.

Fawcett, G.; Stonner, D.; and Zepelin, H. "Locus of Control, Perceived Constraint, and Morale among Institutionalized Aged." *International Journal of Aging and Human Development* 11 (1980):13–23.

Feder, J., and Scanlon, W. "Regulating the Bed Supply in Nursing Homes." *Milbank Memorial Fund Quarterly/Health and Society* 58 (1980):55–88.

Felton, B., and Kahana, E. "Adjustment and Situationally-Bound Locus of Control among Institutionalized Aged." *Journal of Gerontology* 29 (1974):295–301.

Filer, R.N., and O'Connell, D. "Motivation of Aging Persons." *Journal of Gerontology* 19 (1964):15–22.

Fontana, A. *The Last Frontier: The Social Meaning of Growing Old.* Beverly Hills, Calif.: Sage, 1978.

Francis, G., and Odell, S.H. "Long-Term Residence and Loneliness: Myth or Reality?" *Journal of Gerontological Nursing* 5 (1979):9–11.

Garvin, R.M., and Burger, R.E. *Where They Go to Die: The Tragedy of America's Aged.* New York: Delacorte Press, 1968.

Geiger, H.J. "The Causes of Dehumanization in Health Care and Prospects for Humanization." In *Humanizing Health Care,* edited by J. Howard and A. Strauss, pp. 11–36. New York: Wiley, 1975.

Gelfand, D.E. "Visiting Patterns and Social Adjustment in an Old Age Home." *Gerontologist* 8 (1968):272–275.

Gelwicks, L. "Needs, Environmental Design and Health Care of the Aged." In *Psychosocial Needs of the Aged: A Health Care Perspective,* edited by E. Seymour, pp. 29–34. Los Angeles: Ethel Percy Andrus Gerontology Center, University of Southern California, 1978.

George, L.K. *Quality of Care in Nursing Homes: Attitudinal and Environmental Factors.* Durham, N.C.: Duke University, 1979.

Gibson, F.K., and Tinsley, C.E. "The Humanistic Model of Organizational Motivation: A Review of Research Report." *Public Administration Review* 33 (1973):89–95.

Glasscote, R.M. "Old Folks at Homes: Observations and Recommendations." *Journal of Nursing Care* 12 (1979):17–22.

Goffman, E. *Asylums.* Garden City, N.Y.: Doubleday, 1961.

Goldfarb, A.I., and Dobrof, R. *Aged Patients in Long-Term Care Facilities: A Staff Manual.* Washington, D.C.: Government Printing Office, 1973.

Goldstucker, J.L.; Bellenger, D.L.; and Miller, F.D. "A Case Study of the Buying Participant in the Purchase of Nursing Home Services." *Journal of Long-Term Care Administration* 2 (1974):5–19.

Gottesman, L.E. "Milieu Treatment of the Aged in Institutions." *Gerontologist* 13 (1973):23–26.

———. "Nursing Home Performance as Related to Resident Traits, Ownership, Size, and Source of Payment." *American Journal of Public Health* 64 (1974):269–276.

Gottesman, L.E., and Bourestom, N.C. "Why Nursing Homes Do What They Do." *Gerontologist* 14 (1974):501–506.

Green, Z.E. *Depression in the Long-Term Care Facility.* Denton: Center for Studies in Aging, North Texas State University, 1979.

Greenwald, S.R., and Linn, M.W. "Intercorrelation of Data on Nursing Homes." *Gerontologist* 11 (1971):337–340.

Gubrium, J.F. *Living and Dying at Murray Manor.* New York: St. Martin's Press, 1975.

———. "Notes on the Social Organization of Senility." *Urban Life* 7 (1978):23–43.

———. "Patient Exclusion in Geriatric Staffings." *Sociological Quarterly* 21 (1980):335–347.

Gulledge, K. *In-Service Training: How and Why for Long-Term Care Facilities.* Denton: Center for Studies in Aging, North Texas State University, 1977.

Gustafson, D.H.; Fiss, C.J.; Fryback, J.C.; Smelser, P.A.; and Hiles, M.E. "Measuring the Quality of Care in Nursing Homes: A Pilot Study in Wisconsin." *Public Health Reports* 95 (1980):336–343.

Gustafson, E. "Dying: The Career of the Nursing Home Patient." *Journal of Health and Social Behavior* 13 (1972):226–235.

Harel, Z., and Kahana, E. "Social and Behavioral Principles in Residential Care for the Aged." *American Journal of Orthopsychiatry* 42 (1972):331–333.

Harris, J.E., and Bodden, J.L. "An Activity Group Experience for Disengaged Elderly Persons." *Journal of Counseling Psychology* 25 (1978):325–330.

Hatton, J. "Nurse's Attitude toward the Aged: Relationship to Nursing Care." *Journal of Gerontological Nursing* 3 (1977):21–26.

Hinkley, N.E. "Sexuality and Aging: Implications for Long-Term Care." Paper presented at the annual meeting of the Gerontological Society, Washington, D.C., 1979.

Hochschild, A.R. *The Unexpected Community.* Berkeley: University of California Press, 1973.

Hoffman, D.J. "A Health Center but also a Home." *Journal of Gerontological Nursing* 5 (1979):25–28.

Holland, T.P.; Konick, A.; Buffum, W.; Smith, M.K.; and Petchers, M. "Institutional Structure and Resident Outcomes." *Journal of Health and Social Behavior,* in press.

Holmberg, R.H., and Anderson, N.N. "Implications of Ownership for Nursing Home Care." *Medical Care* 6 (1968):300–307.

Holzman, S., and Sabel, E.N. "Improving the Morale of the Patients and

the Staff in a Geriatric Institution by a Supervised Visiting Program."
Gerontologist 8 (1968):29–33.

Howard, J. "Humanization and Dehumanization of Health Care." In
Humanizing Health Care, edited by J. Howard and A. Strauss, pp.
57–107. New York: Wiley, 1975.

Howard, J., and Strong, K.E. "Evaluating the Quality of Nursing Home
Care." *Journal of the American Geriatrics Society* 25 (1977):525–526.

———. "Nurses' Notes on Nursing Home Patients: Are They Effective?"
Journal of the American Geriatrics Society 26 (1978):188–189.

Howard, J.B.; Strong, K.E., Sr.; and Strong, K.E., Jr. "Medication Procedures in a Nursing Home: Abuse of PRN Orders." *Journal of the
American Geriatrics Society* 25 (1977):83–84.

Ingram, D.K., and Barry, J.R. "National Statistics on Deaths in Nursing
Homes: Interpretations and Implications." *Gerontologist* 17 (1977):
303–308.

Jacobs, R.H. "One-Way Street: An Intimate View of Adjustment to a
Home for the Aged." *Gerontologist* 9 (1969):268–275.

Jandel, R.L. "The Job Satisfaction Gap—Where Are We, and Where
Could We Be?" In *Proceedings of the Fourth North American Sym-
posium on Long-Term Care Administration,* edited by American
College of Nursing Home Administrators, pp. 67–77. Washington,
D.C., 1979.

Jessum, K.L. "The Effects of Group Counseling on Geriatric Patients Institutionalized in Long-Term Care Facilities." Ph.D. dissertation, University of Southern California.

Joint Commission on Accreditation of Hospitals. *Accreditation Manual for
Long Term Care Facilities.* Chicago, Ill.: 1979.

Jones, D.C. "Social Isolation, Interaction, and Conflict in Two Nursing
Homes." *Gerontologist* 12 (1972):230–234.

Jorgensen, L.B. and Kane, R.L. "Social Work in the Nursing Home: A
Need and an Opportunity." *Social Work in Health Care* 1 (1976):471–
482.

Kahana, E. Effects of Matching Institutional Environments and Needs of
the Aged." *Gerontologist* 11 (1971):47.

———. "Emerging Issues in Institutional Services for the Aging." *Gerontologist* 11 (1971):51–58.

———. "The Humane Treatment of Old People in Institutions." *Gerontologist* 13 (1973):282–289.

———. "Matching Environments to Needs of the Aged: A Conceptual
Scheme." In *Late Life: Recent Developments in the Sociology of
Aging,* edited by J. Gubrium, pp. 210–214. Springfield, Il.: Charles C
Thomas, 1975.

Kahana, E., and Coe, R.M. "Self and Staff Conceptions of Institutionalized Aged." *Gerontologist* 9 (1969):264–267.

Kahana, E.; Liang, J.; and Felton, B.J. "Alternative Models of Person-Environment Fit: Prediction of Morale in Three Homes for the Aged." *Journal of Gerontology* 35 (1980):584–595.

Kahn, K.A.; Hines, W.; Woodson, A.S.; and Burkham-Armstrong, G. "A Multidisciplinary Approach to Assessing the Quality of Care in Long-Term Care Facilities." *Gerontologist* 17 (1977):61–65.

Kalson, L. "M*A*S*H: A Program of Social Interaction between Institutionalized Aged and Adult Mentally Retarded Persons." *Gerontologist* 16 (1976):340–348.

Kane, R.L., and Kane, R.A. "Care of the Aged: Old Problems in Need of New Solutions." *Science* 200 (1978):913–919.

Karcher, C.J., and Linden, L.L. "Family Rejection of the Aged and Nursing Home Utilization." *International Journal of Aging and Human Development* 5 (1974):231–244.

Kassel, V. "Sex in Nursing Homes." *Medical Aspects of Human Sexuality* 6 (April 1976):126–131.

Kastenbaum, R., and Candy, S.E. "The 4% Fallacy: A Methodological and Empirical Critique of Extended Care Facility Population Statistics." *International Journal of Aging and Human Development* 4 (1973):15–21.

Kauffman, B.K., and Boyle, G.M. "Family Advisory Council in the Long-Term Care Facility." In *Proceedings of the Fifth North American Symposium on Long-Term Care Administration,* edited by American College of Nursing Home Administrators, pp. 51–60. Washington, D.C., 1980.

Kelen, J.G. "The Effects of Poetry on Elderly Nursing Home Residents." Ph.D. dissertation, University of Utah, 1980.

Kerner, M. "Stresses and Strains on Nursing Home Personnel and the Effects on Residents." In *Mental Health in the Nursing Home: An Educational Approach for Staff,* edited by D. Blau and A.O. Freed, pp. 121–138. Boston: Boston Society for Gerontologic Psychiatry, 1979.

Kiyak, H.A.; Kahana, E.; and Lev, N. "The Role of Informal Norms in Determining Institutional Totality in Homes for the Aged." *Long Term Care and Health Services Administration Quarterly* 3 (1979):102–110.

Kleban, M.H.; Lawton, M.P.; Brody, E.M.; and Moss, M. "Characteristics of Mentally Impaired Aged Profiting from Individualized Treatment." *Journal of Gerontology* 30 (1975):90–96.

Klonoff, R. "The Problems of Nursing Homes: Connecticut's Non-Response." *Administrative Law Review* 31 (1979):1–30.

Koncelik, J.A. *Designing the Open Nursing Home.* Stroudsburg, Pa.: Dowden, Hutchinson & Ross, 1976.

Konz, T.R. "Patient Care in Long-Term Care Facilities." *Journal of Long-Term Care Administration* 9 (1981):13–21.

Kosberg, J.I. "Differences in Proprietary Institutions Caring for Affluent and Nonaffluent Elderly." *Gerontologist* 13 (1973):299–304.

———. "Making Institutions Accountable: Research and Policy Issues. *Gerontologist* 14 (1974):510–516.

Kosberg, J.I., and Tobin, S.S. "Variability among Nursing Homes." *Gerontologist* 12 (1972):214–219.

Kragnes, E.N. "Religion in the Lives of Older Persons." In *Long Term Care of the Aging: A Socially Responsible Approach,* edited by L.J. Wasser, pp. 62–66. Washington, D.C.: American Association of Homes for the Aging, 1979.

Kroelinger, M.D. "The Nursing Home as a Living Environment: Resident Satisfaction in Relation to Demographic, Health, and Social-Psychological Factors." Ph.D. dissertation, University of Tennessee, 1977.

Laird, C. *Limbo.* Novato, Calif.: Chandler & Sharp, 1979.

Langer, E.J., and Rodin, J. "The Effects of Choice and Enhanced Personal Responsibility for the Aged: A Field Experiment in an Institutional Setting." *Journal of Personality and Social-Psychology* 34 (1976):191–198.

Lawton, M.P. "Ecology and Aging." In *Spatial Behavior of Older People,* edited by L.A. Pastalan and D.H. Carson, pp. 40–67. Ann Arbor, Mich.: Wayne State Institute of Gerontology, 1970.

———. "Institutions and Alternatives for Older People." *Health and Social Work* 3 (1978):108–133.

Lawton, M.P., and Bader, J. "Wish for Privacy by Young and Old." *Journal of Gerontology* 25 (1970):48–54.

Lee, G.R. "Children and the Elderly: Interaction and Morale." *Research on Aging* 1 (1979):335–360.

Lee, G.R., and Ihinger-Tallman, M. "Sibling Interaction and Morale: The Effects of Family Relations on Older People." *Research on Aging* 2 (1980):367–391.

Lemke, S., and Moos, R.H. "The Suprapersonal Environment of Sheltered Care Settings." *Journal of Gerontology* 36 (1981):233–243.

Lemon, B.W.; Bengtson, V.L.; and Peterson, J.A. "An Exploration of the Activity Theory of Aging: Activity Types and Life Satisfaction among In-Movers to a Retirement Community. *Journal of Gerontology* 27 (1972):511–523.

Lester, P.B., and Baltes, M.M. "Functional Interdependence of the Social Environment and the Behavior of the Institutionalized Aged." *Journal of Gerontological Nursing* 4 (1978):23–27.

Lewis, C.N. "The Adaptive Value of Reminiscing in Old Age." *Journal of Geriatric Psychiatry* 6 (1973):117-121.

Lewis, K. "Practical Illustrations of Nurse-Social Worker Collaboration and Teamwork in a Long-Term Health Care Facility." Journal of Gerontological Nursing 5 (1979):34-39.

Lewis, M.I., and Butler, R.N. "Life-Review Therapy: Putting Memories to Work in Individual and Group Psychotherapy." *Geriatrics* 29 (1974): 165-173.

Liang, J.; Dvorkin, L.; Kahana, E.; and Mazian, F. "Social Integration and Morale, a Re-Examination." *Journal of Gerontology* 35 (1980): 746-757.

Lieberman, M.A. "Institutionalization of the Aged: Effects on Behavior." *Journal of Gerontology* 24 (1969):330-340.

Lieberman, M.A., and Lakin, M. "On Becoming an Institutionalized Aged Person." In *Processes of Aging,* edited by R.H. Williams; C. Tibbitts; and W. Donahue, pp. 475-503. New York: Atherton, 1963.

Linn, M.W. "Predicting Quality of Patient Care in Nursing Homes." *Gerontologist* 14 (1974):225-227.

Linn, M.W., and Gurel, L. "Initial Reactions to Nursing Home Placement." *Journal of the American Geriatrics Society* 17 (1969):219-223.

Linn, M.W.; Gurel, L'.; and Linn, B.S. "Patient Outcome as a Measure of Quality of Nursing Home Care." *American Journal of Public Health* 67 (1977):337-344.

Linn, M.W., and Linn, B.S. "The Public Health Issues in Nursing Home Care." *Public Health Reviews* 8 (1979):177-197.

Linnane, P.D. *Ombudsman for Nursing Homes: Structure and Process.* Washington, D.C.: Government Printing Office, 1975.

Linsk, N.; Howe, M.W., and Pinkston, E.M. "Behavior Group Work in a Home for the Aged." *Social Work* 20 (1975):454-463.

Livengood, M. "A Group-Process Approach to Residents and Staff Abuse." *American Health Care Association Journal* 6 (1980):29-35.

Loeser, W.D.; Dickstein, E.S.; Gilchrist, V.J.; and Weiss, G. "Federal Regulation of Medical Practice in Nursing Homes." *Forum on Medicine* 3 (1980):512-514.

Longenberger, R.F. "Sex and the Elderly." *Journal of Long-Term Care Administration* 8 (1980):13-20.

Lowenthal, M.F., and Simon, A. "Mental Crises and Institutionalization among the Aged." *Journal of Geriatric Psychiatry* 4 (1971):163-187.

Manard, B.B.; Woehle, R.E.; and Heilman, J.M. *Better Homes for the Old.* Lexington, Mass.: D.C. Heath and Company, Lexington, 1977.

Maschiocchi, C.; Poulshock, S.W.; and Brody, S.J. "Impairment Levels of Ill Elderly: Institutional and Community Perspectives." Paper presented at the annual meeting of the American Gerontological Society, 1979.

Maslow, A. *Toward a Psychology of Being.* New York: D. Van Nostrand, 1962.

McCarthy, P. "Geriatric Sexuality: Capacity, Interest, and Opportunity." *Journal of Gerontological Nursing* 5 (1979):20–24.

McClannahan, L.E., and Risley, T.R. "A Store for Nursing Home Residents." *Nursing Homes* 22 (1973):10–29.

————. "Design of Living Environments for Nursing Home Residents." *Gerontologist* 14 (1974):236–240.

————. "Design of Living Environments for Nursing Home Residents: Increasing Participation in Recreation Activities." Journal of Applied Behavior Analysis 8 (1975):261–268.

McMeekin, B. *Family Involvement in the Nursing Home Experience.* Denton: Center for Studies in Aging, North Texas State University, 1977.

Mech, A.B. "Evaluating the Process of Nursing Care in Long-Term Care Facilities." *Quality Review Bulletin* 6 (1980):24–30.

Meditz, J., and Bolton, N. "The Development and Testing of a Process-Outcome Evaluation Instrument Measuring Quality of Care in Nursing Homes as Perceived by Residents." Paper presented at the annual meeting of the American Gerontological Society, 1980.

Melillo, K.D. "Informal Activity Involvement and the Perceived Rate of Time Passage for an Older Institutionalized Population." *Journal of Gerontological Nursing* 6 (1980):392–397.

Mercer, S.D. "Helplessness and Hopelessness in the Institutionalized Aged: A Field Experiment on the Impact of Increased Control and Choice." Ph.D. dissertation, University of Utah, 1978.

Mercer, S.D., and Kane, R.A. "Helplessness and Hopelessness among the Institutionalized Aged: An Experiment." *Health and Social Work* 4 (1979):91–115.

Miller, D.B. "Sexual Practices and Administrative Policies in Long-Term Care Institutions." *Proceedings of the First North American Symposium on Long Term Care Administration,* edited by American College of Nursing Home Administrators, pp. 257–263. Washington, D.C., 1975.

Miller, D.B., and Barry, J.T. "The Relationship of Off-Premises Activities to the Quality of Life of Nursing Home Patients." *Gerontologist* 16 (1976):61–64.

————. "Sexual Activity in the Nursing Home: Patients' Prerogatives versus Personnel Permission." In *Proceedings of the Fifth North American Symposium on Long-Term Care Administration,* edited by American College of Nursing Home Administrators, pp. 85–94. Washington, D.C., 1980.

Miller, D.B., and Beer, S. "Patterns of Friendship among Patients in a Nursing Home Setting." *Gerontologist* 17 (1977):269–275.

Miller, M.B. "Laws and Regulations Detrimental to Quality Care in the Nursing Home." In *Proceedings of the Fourth North American Symposium on Long-Term Care Administration,* edited by American College of Nursing Home Administrators, pp. 94–114. Washington, D.C., 1979.

Miller, P., and Russell, D.A. "Elements Promoting Satisfaction as Identified by Residents in the Nursing Home." *Journal of Gerontological Nursing* 6 (1980):121–129.

Miller, W.R.; Hurley, S.J.; and Wharton, E. "External Peer Review of Skilled Nursing Care in Minnesota." *American Journal of Public Health* 66 (1976):278–283.

Minnix, W.L., Jr. "The Staff's Role in the Long Term Care Facility." In *Long Term Care of the Aging: A Socially Responsible Approach,* edited by L.J. Wasser, pp. 19–22. Washington, D.C., 1979.

Mitchell, J.B. "Patient Outcomes in Alternative Long-Term Care Settings." *Medical Care* 16 (1978):439–452.

Monk, A., and Kaye, L.W. *Ombudsman Services for the Aged in Long Term Care Facilities.* New York: Brookdale Institute on Aging and Adult Human Development, Columbia University, 1981.

Moos, R.H.; Gauvin, M.; Lemke, S.; Max, W.; and Mehren, B. "Assessing the Social Environments of Sheltered Care Settings." *Gerontologist* 19 (1979):74–82.

Moran, J.A. "The Effects of Insight-Oriented Group Therapy and Task-Oriented Group Therapy on the Coping Style and Life Satisfaction of Nursing Home Elderly." Ph.D. dissertation, University of Maryland, 1978.

Moss, F.E. "The Future of Nursing Homes in America." *Institute for Socioeconomic Studies Journal* 3 (1978):28–38.

Moss, F.E., and Halamandaris, V.J. *Too Old, Too Sick, Too Bad: Nursing Homes in America.* Germantown, Md.: Aspen, 1977.

Mullins, L.C. "A Study of the Alienation of Male and Female Nursing Home Patients." *Long Term Care and Health Services Administration Quarterly,* 4 (1980):305–314.

Munley, A.; Powers, C.S.; and Williamson, J.B. "Humanizing Nursing Home Environments: The Relevance of Hospice Principles." Paper presented at the annual meeting of the American Sociological Association, 1980.

Myles, J. "The Bureaucratization of Consumption: Institutional Welfare for the Aged." Paper presented at the annual meeting of the International Sociological Association, 1978.

Myrtle, R.C., and Robertson, J.P. "Developing Work Group Satisfaction:

The Influence of Teams, Team Work and the Team Approach." *Long Term Care and Health Services Administration Quarterly* 3 (1979): 149–164.

―――. "Determinants of Job Satisfaction in Nursing Care Units." *Journal of Long-Term Care Administration* 7 (1979):17–29.

National Association of Social Workers, "Easing the Strain on Families of Nursing Home Residents." *Practice Digest* 2 (1979a)18–20.

―――. *Long-Term Care for the Elderly, Chronically Ill and Disabled.* Washington, D.C., 1979b.

Nicholson, C.K. "Personalized Care Model." Unpublished paper. Syracuse University, Syracuse, N.Y., no date.

―――. "Personalized Patient Care in the Nursing Home: Problems and Practice." Paper presented at the annual meeting of the Gerontological Society, 1979.

Noam, E. *Homes for the Aged: Supervision and Standards.* Translated by J.S. Monks. Washington, D.C.: Government Printing Office, 1975.

Novick, L.J. "Staff Coordination in a Long-Term Geriatric Hospital." *Long-Term Care and Health Services Administration Quarterly* 4 (1980):115–124.

Ober, B. *Residents' Clothing: A Challenge for Family, Staff, and Administrator in the Nursing Home.* Denton: Center for Studies in Aging, North Texas State University, 1979.

Ostrander, E.R. "Research Based Nursing Home Design: An Approach for Planning Environments for the Aging." *International Journal of Aging and Human Development* 4 (1973):307–317.

Peace, S. "'Small Group Living' in Institutional Settings." *Aging International* 8 (1981):13–16.

Pecarchik, R., and Nelson, B.H., Jr. "Employee Turnover in Nursing Homes." *Journal of the American College of Nursing Home Administrators* 1 (1973):27–31.

Penchansky, R., and Taubenhaus, L.J. "Institutional Factors Affecting the Quality of Care in Nursing Homes." *Geriatrics* 20 (1965):591–598.

Phillips, J.R. "Music in the Nursing of Elderly Persons in Nursing Homes." *Journal of Gerontological Nursing* 6 (1980):37–39.

Pincus, A., and Wood, V. "Methodological Issues in Measuring the Environment in Institutions for the Aged and Its Impact on Residents." International Journal of Aging and Human Development 1 (1970): 117–126.

Posner, J. "Notes on the Negative Implications of Being Competent in a Home for the Aged." *International Journal of Aging and Human Development* 5 (1974):357–364.

Poulshock, S.W.; Masciocchi, C.; and Brody, S.J. "Differential Characteristics of Nursing Home Residents in Proprietary, Voluntary, and

Public Homes." Paper presented at the annual meeting of the Gerontological Society, 1979.

Power, C.A., and McCarron, L.P. "Treatment of Depression in Persons Residing in Homes for the Aged." *Gerontologist* 15 (1975):132–135.

Pringle, B.M. "Housing Living Arrangements for the Elderly: Some Ideas from Northern Europe." *Housing and Society* 5 (1978):20–25.

Proctor, S. *In-Service Training: Role and Structure in Long-Term Care Facilities.* Denton: Center for Studies in Aging, North Texas State University, 1976.

Purcell, M. "Foster Grandparents in a Residential Treatment Center." *Child Welfare* 58 (1979):409–411.

Rebok, G.W., and Hoyer, W.J. "The Functional Context of Elderly Behavior." *Gerontologist* 17 (1977):27–34.

Reiff, T.R. "When a Patient Is Admitted to a Nursing Home." *Geriatrics* 35 (1980):87–94.

Reiner, A. "Ethnic Music in Music Therapy: A Program for Jewish Geriatric Residents." *Long Term Care and Health Services Administration Quarterly* 3 (1979):301–306.

Reitzes, A.G. "The Forms of Social Interaction of Older People." Ph.D. dissertation, University of Maryland, 1978.

Riskin, C. "Activity Programs in Homes for the Aged." In *Long Term Care of the Aging: A Socially Responsible Approach,* edited by L.J. Wasser, pp. 55–61. Washington, D.C.: American Association of Homes for the Aging, 1979.

Robb, J.W. "Analysis of Choice: Value-Conflict." *Journal of Long Term Care Administration* 4 (1976):14–28.

Romney, L.S. "Extension of Family Relationships into a Home for the Aged." *Social Work* 7 (1962):31–34.

Ronch, J.L., and Maizler, J.S. "Individual Psychotherapy with the Institutionalized Aged." *American Journal of Orthopsychiatry,* 47 (1977): 275–283.

Rose, A.M. "Mental Health of Normal Older Persons." *Geriatrics* 16 (1961):459–464.

―――. "A Current Theoretical Issue in Social Gerontology." In *Middle Age and Aging,* edited by B. Newgarten, pp. 29–34. Chicago: University of Chicago Press, 1968.

Rosenfeld, A.H. *New Views on Older Lives.* Washington, D.C. Government Printing Office, 1978.

Sainsbury, P., and de Alarcon, J.G. "The Psychiatrist and the Geriatric Patient." The Effects of Community Care on the Family of the Geriatric Patient." *Journal of Geriatric Psychiatry* 4 (1970):23–41.

Sancier, B. "Final Report. Family Life Education: A Model Training Program for Social Workers in Long-Term Care Facilities, Nursing Home

Residents and Their Families." University of Wisconsin-Madison, Madison, WI, 1981.

Schneider, F.W., and Coppinger, N.W. "Staff-Resident Perceptions of the Needs and Adjustment of Nursing Home Residents." *Aging and Human Development* 2 (1971):59–65.

Schramm, W., and Storey, R.T. *Little House: A Study of Senior Citizens.* Peninsula Volunteers, Menlo Park, CA, and Institute for Communication Research, Stanford University, Stanford, CA, 1961.

Schwab, M. "Issues in Institutional Care of the Aged." *Excerpta Medica, International Congress Series* 469 (1979):596–599.

Schwenk, M.A. "Reality Orientation for the Institutionalized Aged: Does It Help?" *Gerontologist* 19 (1979):373–377.

Seelbach, W.C., and Hansen, C.J. "Self-Concept among Institutionalized and Non-institutionalized Elderly." *Long Term Care and Health Services Administration Quarterly* 4 (1980):93–102.

Shaughnessy, M.E. "Emotional Problems of Patients in Nursing Homes," *Journal of Geriatric Psychiatry* 1 (1968):159–166.

Sherman, E., and Newman, E.S. "The Meaning of Cherished Personal Possessions for the Elderly." *Journal of Aging and Human Development* 8 (1977–1978):181–192.

Shoemaker, D.M. Dialectics of Nursing Homes and Aging. *Journal of Gerontological Nursing* 5 (1979):45–48.

Shore, H. "Public Policy for Long Term Care." *Long Term Care and Health Services Administration Quarterly* 4 (1980):236–243.

Silverstone, B.M. "Multilevels and Options in Chronic Care: Myth or Reality?" *Bulletin of the New York Academy of Medicine* 54 (1978): 271–275.

Slater, R., and Lipman, A. "Staff Assessments of Confusion and the Situation of Confused Residents in Homes for Old People." *Gerontologist* 17 (1977):523–530.

Smith, H.L.; Discenza, R.; and Saxberg, B.O. "Nurses' Perspectives of Decision Making in Nursing Homes." *Journal of Long-Term Care Administration* 6 (1978):1–12.

Smith, K.F., and Bengtson, V.L. "Positive Consequences of Institutionalization: Solidarity between Elderly Parents and Their Middle-Aged Children." *Gerontologist* 19 (1979):438–447.

Smith, R.T., and Brand, F.N. "Effects of Enforced Relocation on Life Adjustment in a Nursing Home." *International Journal of Aging and Human Development* 6 (1975):249–259.

Snyder, L.H. "An Exploratory Study of Patterns of Social Interaction, Organization, and Facility Design in Three Nursing Homes." *International Journal of Aging and Human Development* 4 (1973):319–333.

Solomon, J.R. "Outreach Services in God's Waiting Room." *Health and Social Work* 1 (1976):59–70.

Sommer, R. "Small Group Ecology in Institutions for the Elderly." In *Spatial Behavior of Older People,* edited by L.A. Pastalan and D.H. Carson, pp.25–39. Ann Arbor, Mich.: Wayne State Institute of Gerontology, 1970.

Stannard, C.I. "Old Folks and Dirty Work: The Social Conditions for Patient Abuse in a Nursing Home." *Social Problems* 20 (1973):329–341.

Stone, V. "Patient Care Assessment: A Managerial Strategy." *Journal of Long-Term Care Administration* 2 (1974):18–24.

Streib, G.F., and Hilker, M.A. "The Cooperative 'Family': An Alternative Life Style for the Elderly." *Alternative Lifestyles* 3 (1980):167–184.

Tate, J.W. "The Need for Personal Space in Institutions for the Elderly." *Journal of Gerontological Nursing* 6 (1980):439–449.

Taylor, K.H., and Harned, T.L. "Attitudes toward Old People: A Study of Nurses Who Care for the Elderly." *Journal of Gerontological Nursing* 4 (1978):43–47.

Tec, N., and Granick, R. "Social Isolation and Difficulties in Social Interaction of Residents of a Home for the Aged." *Social Problems* 7 (1959–1960):226–232.

Terman, L.A. "Selecting A 'Home' for the Elderly and Chronically Ill." *Geriatrics* 20 (1965):599–603.

Teski, N. *Living Together: Ethnography of a Retirement Hotel.* Washington, D.C.: University Press of America, 1979.

Tillock, E.E. "The Humane Environment in Nursing Home Care." *Nursing Homes* 28 (1979):22–24.

Tillock, E.E., and Zaso, G.C. "Administrative Implications for Recreational Services in Long Term Care Facilities." *Long Term Care and Health Services Administration Quarterly* 2 (1978):292–299.

Tobin, S.S. "The Mystique of Deinstitutionalization." *Society* 15 (1978):73–75.

Tobin, S.S., and Lieberman, M.A. *Last Home for the Aged.* San Francisco: Jossey-Bass, 1976.

Toseland, R.W. "Rehabilitation and Discharge: The Nursing Home Dilemma." *Long Term Care and Health Services Administration Quarterly* 3 (1979):284–300.

Townsend, C. *Old Age: The Last Segregation.* New York: Grossman, 1971.

Townsend, P. *The Last Refuge: A Survey of Residential Institutions and Homes for the Aged in England and Wales.* London: Routledge & Kegan Paul, 1962.

———. "The Purpose of the Institution." In *Social and Psychological*

Aspects of Aging, edited by C. Tibbitts and W. Donahue, pp. 378–399. New York: Columbia University Press, 1962.

Trierweiler, R. "Personal Space and Its Effects on an Elderly Individual in a Long-Term Care Institution." *Journal of Gerontological Nursing* 4 (1978):21–23.

Turner, B.F.; Tobin, S.S.; and Lieberman, M.A. "Personalities Traits as Predictors of Institutional Adaptation among the Aged." *Journal of Gerontology* 27 (1972):61–68.

Turner, J. "The Last Refuges, Where All Too Many Old People Go to Die." *New Society* 47 (1979):183–186.

Tverskoy, I. "USSR: Nursing Homes for the Aged." *Journal of Gerontological Nursing* 4 (1978):14–17.

U.S. Senate. Special Committee on Aging. *Nursing Home Care in the United States: Failure in Public Policy. Supporting Paper No. 6: What Can be Done in Nursing Homes: Positive Aspects in Long-Term Care.* Washington, D.C.: Government Printing Office, 1975.

Vail, D.J. *Dehumanization in the Institutional Career.* Springfield, Ill.: Charles C Thomas, 1966.

Vladeck, B.C. *Unloving Care: The Nursing Home Tragedy.* New York: Basic Books, 1980.

Volinn, I.J. "Institutionalized Aged: A Research Review." *Public Health Reviews* 6 (1977):37–60.

Wallach, H.F.; Kelley, F.; and Abrahams, J.P. "Psychological Rehabilitation for Chronic Geriatric Patients: An Intergenerational Approach." *Gerontologist* 9 (1979):464–470.

Wasow, M., and Loeb, N.B. "Sexuality in Nursing Homes." *Journal of the American Geriatrics Society* 27 (1979):73–79.

Waters, J.E. "Assessing the Work Environment of Long Term Health Care Facilities." *Long Term Care and Health Services Administration Quarterly* 2 (1978):300–307.

———. "The Social Ecology of Long-Term Care Facilities for the Aged: A Case Example." *Journal of Gerontological Nursing* 6 (1980):155–160.

Watson, W.H. "Body Image and Staff-to-Resident Deportment in a Home for the Aged." *International Journal of Aging and Human Development* 1 (1970):345–359.

———. "Institutional Structures of Aging and Dying." In *Environmental Research and Aging,* edited by Gerontological Society, pp. 39–65. Washington, D.C., 1974.

———. "The Meanings of Touch: Geriatric Nursing." *Journal of Communication* 37 (1975):107–127.

Weinberg, J. "What Do I Say to My Mother When I Have Nothing To Say?" *Geriatrics* 29 (1974):155–159.

Wells, L., and Macdonald, G. "Interpersonal Networks and Post-relocation Adjustment of the Institutionalized Elderly." *Gerontologist* 21 (1981):177-183.

Wentzel, M.L. *The Emotional Effect of Parental Institutionalization upon the Family.* Denton: Center for Studies in Aging, North Texas State University, 1979.

Wetzel, J.W. "Interventions with the Depressed Elderly in Institutions." *Social Casework* 61 (1980):234-239.

White, B.F.; Larocca, P.; and Weeks, J.C. *Conducting Communitywide Nursing Home Inventories: A Citizens Guide.* Washington, D.C.: Urban Institute, 1977.

White, C.M. "The Nurse-Patient Encounter: Attitudes and Behaviors in Action." *Journal of Gerontological Nursing* 3 (1977):16-20.

Wigdor, R.N.; Nelson, J.; and Hickerson, E. "The Behavioral Comparison of a Real vs. Mock Nursing Home." Paper presented at the annual meeting of the Gerontological Society, 1977.

Wilson, S.H. "Nursing Home Patients' Rights: Are They Enforceable?" *Gerontologist* 18 (1978):255-261.

Winn, S., and Kessler, S. "Community Mental Health Centers and the Nursing Home Patient." *Gerontologist* 14 (1974):345-348.

York, J.L., and Calsyn, R.J. "Family Involvement in Nursing Homes." *Gerontologist* 17 (1977):500-505.

Zeisel, J.; Epp, G.; and Demos, S. *Low Rise Housing for Older People: Behavioral Criteria for Design.* Washington, D.C.: Government Printing Office, 1977.

Index

About the Author

Lee H. Bowker is the associate dean of the School of Social Welfare at the University of Wisconsin—Milwaukee. He is the author of *Prisoner Subcultures* (Lexington Books, 1977); *Women, Crime, and the Criminal Justice System* (Lexington Books, 1978); *Women and Crime in America; Prison Victimization;* and *Corrections: The Science and the Art.* He has also published articles in such journals as *Crime and Delinquency, International Journal of Women's Studies, Adolescence, Victimology, The International Journal of Comparative and Applied Criminal Justice,* the *United Nations Bulletin on Narcotics,* and *Liberal Education.* His current interests are in the structure of academic disciplines, behavior and administration in institutions, sex roles and sexual oppression, and geriatric service-delivery systems.